SHAPING THE EASTER FEAST

What Is Normative About Easter?

SHAPING THE EASTER FEAST

Anscar J. Chupungco, O.S.B.

The Pastoral Press
Washington, DC

ISBN: 0-912405-95-3

The Pastoral Press
225 Sheridan Street, NW
Washington, DC 20011
(202) 723-1254

The Pastoral Press is the Publications division of the National Association
of Pastoral Musicians, a membership organization of musicians and clergy
dedicated to fostering the art of musical liturgy.

Printed in the United States of America.

Contents

For the Benedictine Monks of Manila

Foreword

Early in 1992 the U.S. National Aeronautics and Space Administration released the findings from atmospheric studies which indicated that the ozone layer in northernmost regions in the United States, Canada, Europe, and Russia could be depleted by as much as forty percent. This has caused alarm in the developed countries and is one more indication of the long-term insensitivity of the earthlings of the industrialized age to the cosmic life-support system that governs earthly existence.

An unexpected by-product of the commemoration of the fifth centenary of the arrival of Columbus in the New World is the interest and studies in Pre-Columbian "Americans." These original inhabitants of the American continents had based their life and built their civilizations on a sensitive recognition of the life-support system governing the cosmos. This sensitivity is captured in the recorded address of Seattle, chief of the Dwamish, upon surrendering his land to Gov. Isaac Stevens in 1854. Part of his address runs:

> This we know, the earth does not belong to man,
> man belongs to the earth.
> This we know, all things are connected
> like the blood that unites one family.
> All things are connected.
> Whatever befalls the earth,
> befalls the sons of the earth.
> Man did not weave the web of life,
> he is merely a strand in it.
> Whatever he does to the web,
> he does to himself.

In a scholarly study, Fr. Anscar Chupungco, O.S.B., has traced the "relation of the Easter celebration to the cosmic elements . . . such as spring, spring equinox, and full moon." This study has focused attention on the truth that "nature and time were not only signs of God's dealings with people, they were symbols that embodied, manifested, and brought along his salvation."

In tracing early Christianity's determination to set the Easter celebration after the spring equinox, Fr. Chupungco reminds us that springtime "brings to mind everything that Passover signifies: creation, new birth, renewal of life." The cosmic elements of Easter are not just the author's speculations. Going through the Jewish antecedents of Passover, the texts of the sacred word, the patristic writings, and the documents of the church, the author shows us that the celebration of new life brought by the resurrection of Jesus is intricately woven by cosmic strands.

At a time when the inhabitants of the earth are moving toward a more pervasive recognition and acceptance of the interrelation of all life-forms and energies, Fr. Anscar Chupungco joins the multitude of voices crying for us to open the vistas and horizons of our thinking to the life linking the universe. As the popular verses of Amanda Bradly put it:

> The sleeping earth awakens,
> the robins start to sing,
> The flowers open wide their eyes
> to tell us it is spring.
> The bleakness of the winter
> is melted by the sun,
> The tree that looked so stark and dead
> becomes a living one.
> These miracles of Easter
> wrought with divine perfection
> Are the blessed reassurance
> of our Savior's Resurrection.

Abbot Andres Formilleza, O.S.B.
Abbey of Our Lady of Montserrat
Manila, Philippines

Introduction

LITURGICAL FEASTS WITNESS TO THE CHURCH'S INCARNATION IN CULTURE AND
the cosmos. Some feasts evoke religious and secular traditions, the cycle of human labor, and the ever-changing systems of politics and ideology. Others, on the other hand, are seasonal, that is, they are associated with the seasonal turning points of the year. Examples of these feasts are Easter, Pentecost, Christmas, Epiphany, Presentation, Birthday of John the Baptist, and probably St. Michael the Archangel. None of them, however, possesses a date, a theology, and a liturgy with as much cosmic underpinning as Easter. Both the origin and evolution of this feast reveal such cosmic influence as no other seasonal feast is able to claim.

Yet Easter is Christianity's most spiritual feast. Its cosmic elements do not obscure its spiritual character; rather, they enhance it. Nature is one of the eloquent symbols of the presence in our world of Christ's suffering, death, and resurrection. However, in many people such a view of nature is sadly impaired, if not lost, because of purely materialistic approaches to God's creation. We have to rediscover the sacramental character of nature, if we wish to experience the mystery of Christ.

This volume, whose aim is to make a contribution to that rediscovery, is an enlarged and revised version of my book *The Cosmic Elements of Christian Passover* which appeared in *Studia Anselmiana*, vol. 72 (Rome) in 1977. The book has been out of print since 1985. In the process of revision I added a new chapter and rewrote the old material. I also updated the bibliography and elaborated topics that relate to the question of inculturation. On the whole this volume can be considered a new book.

I am grateful to the administrators of *Studia Anselmiana* for granting permission to publish this new version with The Pastoral Press.

I am grateful to my Benedictine community of Manila for giving me all the time I needed to work on this volume, and to Rev. Gerald Shirilla for encouraging me to undertake the tedious task of revising an earlier work.

Paul VI Institute of Liturgy
Malaybalay, Philippines

Chapter One
The Meaning of Easter

A Definition of Easter

CHRISTIAN TRADITION HAS ALWAYS ASSOCIATED THE FEAST OF EASTER WITH THE Jewish feast of Passover. The association is generally based on an ancient system of types and antitypes. According to this system of thought the Jewish feast was the type or prefiguration of Christian Easter. Hence the death and resurrection of Christ was the antitype which marked the fulfillment of the prophetic Jewish Passover. In Christian thinking the paschal lamb, whose blood spared the Israelites from death at the time of the exodus, signified the person of Christ, the true lamb of God, whose sacrifice redeemed us from the slavery of sin. His death on the cross on Good Friday, at the same time as the immolation of the paschal lambs in the temple precinct of Jerusalem, came to be understood as the new exodus, the new Passover. Finally, the crossing of the sea by the fleeing Israelites was likewise interpreted as his passage through the "waters of death" to the glory of the resurrection.

The parallelism between the Jewish exodus and Christ's sacrificial death was a favorite topic among early Christian homilists. But it is particularly sharpened by the church's minute observance of the Jewish paschal calendar, with the exception of Sunday which is, in a sense, the Christian counterpart of the Jewish fourteenth day of Nisan. Just as the event of the exodus thoroughly permeated the history and institutions of Israel, so the mystery of Christ's sacrifice and resurrection has indelibly left its imprint on the pages of human history for the past two thousand years. Christ's new and permanent exodus alone can satisfactorily explain the steadfast faith of the church, the blood of martyrs, the perseverance of all the Christian saints. St. Paul writes in 1 Corinthians 15:17-18, "if Christ was not raised, your faith is worthless. You are still in your sins, and those who have fallen asleep in Christ are the deadest of the dead."

The traditional teaching of the church on this subject is succinctly expressed by S. Marsili: "When Christ passed from this world to the Father (Jn 13:1), he brought to completion the Jewish Passover, that is, the meaning and force of liberation announced by the prophetic event of exodus. In this way he made his death, resurrection, and ascension the focal point of the history of salvation."[1] Christian theology describes the relationship between the exodus and Christ's paschal mystery in terms of type and antitype, foreshadowing and reality, prophecy and fulfillment.

The feast of Passover was instituted to recall yearly the wonderful deed of God in the exodus. In memory of Christ's redemptive act the yearly feast of Easter was established. While the Jewish Passover, according to Christian theology, looked forward to its own fulfillment in Christ's paschal death and glory, our Easter looks back to them in anamnesis or in ritual memorial. We may say that Christ's cross and resurrection stand between the Jewish Passover and the Christian feast of Easter as the fulfillment of the former and the object of the latter. 1 Corinthians 5:7b-8 is a classic text that aptly connects the different kinds of passover with one another: "Christ our Passover has been sacrificed. Let us celebrate the feast not with the old yeast, that of corruption and wickedness, but with the unleavened bread of sincerity and truth."

This interconnection will be more easily grasped if we compare Easter with the Jewish Passover. Both of them are in fact commemorative rites of a past event. While the Jewish Passover recalled the event of the exodus, Christian Easter commemorates the passage of Christ to glory. Between Christ's passover and our Easter celebration we perceive the same relationship that can be observed between an historical event and its commemorative rite. According to S. Marsili, "our Easter is the ritualization of the event of Christ's death and resurrection."[2] Lastly, just as the Jewish feast foreshadowed the passover of Christ, so our feast is the foretaste of the eternal passover of all those redeemed by the blood of the Lamb.

The feast of Easter falls under the category of a yearly commemoration or anniversary of what Christ has done for us. The idea will become clearer if we view the feast of Easter in the light of Sunday. Whereas Sunday renews the church's weekly encounter with the risen Lord, Easter is the solemn anniversary of his death and resurrection. Whereas Sunday is transformed by the eucharist into the Lord's Day, the feast of Easter is the yearly presence of Christ's paschal mystery shining through, especially in the solemn celebration of the sacraments of initiation during Easter Vigil. The reason is that Easter marks that particular time in the year when the death and resurrection of Christ are reckoned to have taken place around two thousand years ago. This is why it is probably not totally in keeping with liturgical theology to regard Easter merely as another Sunday of the year, even if one grants that its importance and solemnity make the other Sundays seem dim by comparison. Easter is a yearly feast, an anniversary, and the church's scrupulous concern to keep it at the appointed time only confirms the belief of Christians regarding the historical character or historicity of Christ's death on the cross. The other Sundays of the year, since they are not anniversary celebrations, do not possess this particular quality of Easter.

In liturgical usage Easter means either the triduum, with Sunday as the chief referent, or the season of fifty days lasting from Easter Sunday to Pentecost. In this connection, art. 18 of *General Norms for the Liturgical Year and the Calendar* explains that "the Easter triduum of the passion and resurrection of Christ is the culmination of the entire liturgical year. Thus the solemnity of Easter has the same kind of preeminence in the liturgical year that Sunday has in the week."[3] It is important to note that this document calls the Easter triduum the solemnity of Easter. Although in reality Easter encompasses everything relating to Christ's paschal mystery, as a feast or solemnity it refers chiefly to the celebration of the triduum. The triduum itself, according to art. 19 of the same document, "begins with the evening Mass of the Lord's Supper, reaches its high point in the Easter Vigil, and closes with evening prayer on Easter Sunday." This liturgical refinement has not been caught by popular usage which generally confines Easter to Sunday.

There is something theologically profound in the traditional concept of Easter triduum. We refer to the unity it establishes between Christ's death and resurrection. These two saving events are inseparable: they constitute a single mystery. Easter celebrates not only the resurrection but also the cross. This is why the entire triduum is called the sollemnity of Easter. In the course of this work we shall have occasion to address the debate among some early Christian writers regarding the word *pascha* or *transitus*, which we have translated simply as Easter. Does the word embrace both death and resurrection, or is it confined to either one or the other? In the second century we come across a significantly large group of Christians in Asia Minor called Quartodecimans. These interpreted *pascha* to mean the death of Jesus, his passage to the Father. And since the prevailing belief is that he died at the full moon of spring when the paschal lambs were being immolated, they celebrated Easter on that day, regardless of whether or not it was Sunday. The church in the west, on the other hand, laid great stress on the resurrection of Christ which took place on Sunday. This explains why Easter is generally understood as the feast of the resurrection.

The accepted teaching is that Easter as concept and as celebration embraces both the death and glorification of Christ. The Easter triduum, which may be regarded as one prolonged liturgical day, is a fitting embodiment of this theology. St. Ambrose of Milan spoke of the "sacred triduum" or the three days when Christ "suffered, was laid in the tomb, and rose again."[4] St. Augustine also understood the triduum to comprise the three days in solemn remembrance of "Christ crucified, buried, and risen."[5] These days were originally Good Friday, Holy Saturday, and Easter Sunday. When the Roman Church introduced in the seventh century the Mass commemorating the Last Supper, Thursday became part of the triduum, replacing Easter Sunday in the process. The result was disconcerting. The Easter triduum was, contrary to sound tradition, deprived of the Sunday of the resurrection. The reform of Vatican II, whose triduum opens with the evening Mass of Holy Thursday and closes with evening prayer on Easter Sunday, is a worthy compromise and a satisfactory solution to a liturgical problem.[6]

Article 19 of the *General Norms for the Liturgical Year and the Calendar* assigns to the Easter Vigil a central position. Referring to the liturgical practice in the third century, P. Jounel writes:

> At that time the Christian Easter consisted in a fast, a feast, and a transition from the one to the other during a holy night in which the hours of fasting were completed by prayer and in which the feast day was opened by the Eucharist.[7]

The transition between fasting and feasting is what evolved later into the Easter Vigil, a nocturnal celebration that recalls the vigil kept by the Israelites at the time of the exodus, as it keeps the church in prayerful expectation of the Lord's resurrection.

It is not our intention to dwell at any length on the meaning and elements of the Easter Vigil. For our purpose it would suffice to quote the description made by P. Jounel:

> In its content the Easter Vigil is a commemoration of the exodus of the Old Testament people, as well as of the death and resurrection of the Lord; it brings the presence of the risen Christ in the assembly of the people of the new covenant through the sacraments of Christian initiation; and it is a time of waiting for his return, which, it was long thought, would occur precisely during an Easter Vigil.[8]

As regards the liturgical components of the vigil during the first few centuries, A. Nocent gives the following information:

> Three basic elements characterized the Easter Vigil at a very early time: the celebration of the word (first element) which was protracted until the moment of baptism (second element) and the Eucharist (third element) which crowned the entire celebration.[9]

Another consideration on the theology of Easter is its date. Unlike Christmas which has a fixed calendar date, Easter can fall on any Sunday within a period of thirty-five days after the full moon following the spring equinox. This happens because Easter date is the confluence of several cosmic or time elements such as spring, equinox, full moon, and Sunday. Such a confluence is needed because Easter is an anniversary and should, in consequence, be celebrated as close as possible to the historical date of Christ's own passover. The question modern people raise is how to translate this cosmic "date" into calendar date. The answer is that these time elements, which are part of the lunisolar calendar the church uses for this feast, determine the date of Christ's death. Once a year during the week following the spring full moon the church recalls that it was at this time of the year when the Son of God died and rose again. There is something sacred about this "date" because it is related to the church's duty to remember the saving work of Christ. We can understand why Theophilus of Alexandria wrote with authority: "The law of God minutely describes the feast of Easter, indicates the month in which it is to be kept, and prescribes that the date be reckoned with utmost accuracy.[10]

Accuracy in the method of reckoning the Easter date was one of the problems that haunted the early church. Even today it is one of the issues, though reduced to a minor question, that separates the churches. While some churches in the east still adhere to the old Julian calendar for determining the date of Easter, others like the Roman Church have adopted the more accurate Gregorian calendar long ago. The difference between the two calendars can mean a distance of as much as one month between the two resulting dates of Easter. In fact, it rarely happens that churches observing either the Julian or the Gregorian date celebrate Easter at the same time. In the expanse of twenty-five years from 1965 to 2000 there have been only seven such occasions, namely 1966, 1974, 1977, 1980, 1984, 1987, and 1990.

The question of observing a fixed calendar date for the feast of Easter has time and again been raised in and outside the Roman Church. Easter is undeniably a principal entry in programming secular calendars. Its movable date can cause inconvenience to the regular schedule of human activities. Pope Leo XIII in 1897 and Pope Pius XI in 1924 received formal requests from interested groups to support the move for a fixed Easter date. In both instances the Holy See prudently answered that the matter could be decided only by an ecumenical council. It seems that the reticence of the Holy See stemmed from a founded fear that a change in the date of Easter could introduce additional discord among the churches or perhaps even provoke schism, as was verified in the Greek Church when in 1924 it shifted to the Gregorian calendar.[11]

The matter did not rest there. A good number of bishops suggested to the antepreparatory commission of Vatican II that the council should include in its agenda the question of fixing the feast of Easter in the month of April. Some expressed preference for the second Sunday of April. Any proposal in this regard must, of course, take Sunday into account. Because of Sunday, Easter cannot have a fixed date like Christmas. The response of bishops to the antepreparatory commission explains the appendix to the Constitution on the Liturgy. "The Second Vatican Council," the Declaration on Revision of the Calendar states, "recognizes the importance of the wishes expressed by many on assigning the feast of Easter to a fixed Sunday." It furthermore gives the assurance that "the Council is not opposed to the assignment of the feast of Easter to a particular Sunday of the

Gregorian Calendar, provided those whom it may concern, especially other Christians who are not in communion with the Apostolic See, give their assent."[12] This is probably the only issue in the constitution that to date has, for good or ill, remained unattended to.

Easter and the Lord's Day

A striking feature of the postconciliar liturgical calendar is the preference it gives to Sunday over a significant number of other feasts. It would not be unwarranted to ascribe this to the liturgical movement which preceded the council. The first draft of the Constitution on the Liturgy was a faithful echo of what the liturgical movement had been saying all along, namely that Sunday should be reinstated to its rightful place in the liturgical year and estimation of the faithful. The preparatory commission in charge of the draft explained that there was no better way of bringing this about than by instilling in the faithful the value of Sunday observance. In this connection the commission named three doctrinal principles that should be proposed to the consideration of the faithful. First, Sunday is the Lord's Day; second, it commemorates the resurrection of Christ, indeed the whole paschal mystery; and third, it is a day suited for celebrating baptism.[13]

It might seem curious that the preparatory commission made no mention of the Sunday eucharist, the one celebration that should characterize this day. According to S. Marsili, the eucharist is the sacrament whereby the risen Christ appears to the church and which "transforms the first day of the week into the Day of the Lord."[14] It is probable that the commission took this for granted or else implied it in the concept of the Lord's Day. At any rate the final text of the constitution, art. 106, names the eucharist: "On this day Christ's faithful must gather together so that, by hearing the word of God and taking part in the eucharist, they may call to mind the passion, the resurrection, and the glorification of the Lord Jesus." In contrast to the first draft, however, the final text no longer mentions baptism directly, although its quotation from 1 Peter 1:3, which is considered a baptismal catechesis, is probably an allusion to Sunday baptism.

What is noteworthy about this is the way the preparatory commission viewed the connection between Sunday baptism and the commemoration of Christ's resurrection. On Sunday these two things, according to the commission, should be linked together, "in the same manner as on Easter Vigil." It would appear then that the commission regarded the Easter vigil as the paradigm of Sunday liturgy. Are we to conclude from this that the commission was working on a principle which allotted to the Easter Vigil the position of primacy in the liturgical year?

We know that art. 106 of the Constitution on the Liturgy thought otherwise. Tracing the origin of Sunday liturgy to the day when Christ rose from the dead, it speaks of Sunday as "the foundation and core of the whole liturgical year" and "the original feastday" as well, that is, the first in order of time. In the thinking of art. 106 the liturgical year grew from Sunday and evolved into a cycle of weeks with Sunday as the nucleus of all other liturgical feasts. This seems to be the meaning behind the unqualified affirmation that Sunday is the foundation and core of the liturgical year, an affirmation that perhaps needs to be qualified in the light of history. In fact, the first draft of the constitution had another view of the question. It tells us that "the paschal mystery is, as it were, the center and summit of the whole liturgical year." The statement could not be more theologically sound. But in an effort to give ascendancy to Sunday the conciliar commission hastily struck out these words and declared that Sunday is the foundation and core of the liturgical year. Perhaps inadvertently the commission removed from the theology of the liturgical year its very foundation, namely the paschal mystery. The shift from the paschal mystery to Sunday liturgy only shows how far the commission was willing to go in order to enhance the value of Sunday.[15]

Although the preparatory commission advanced the idea that the Easter Vigil is the paradigm of Sunday liturgy, art. 106 of the constitution preferred to give the primacy to Sunday. The chief consideration seems to lie in the theology of Sunday as the day of the resurrection. However, there is another consideration which merits close attention. In the tradition of Rome the memorial of the resurrection is not kept solely in the framework of a weekly cycle. From time immemorial the Church of Rome has been celebrating the paschal mystery, with heavy stress on the resurrection, not only once a week on Sunday but also once a year on Easter Sunday. One could, of course, argue that in the final analysis there is no difference between the two celebrations, since they are both held on Sunday.

There is a difference. While the weekly celebration focuses on the presence and manifestation of the risen Lord on the eighth day, the yearly celebration takes the form of anniversary. Once a year the church solemnly commemorates the events of the paschal mystery at a date reckoned to be closest to the time when these events took place. What emerges clearly from the Quartodeciman controversy during the second century is that the early church already observed two distinct cycles within the liturgical year. One of these was the weekly which centered on Sunday.[16] The other was the yearly which commemorated the death and resurrection of Christ on the assigned Sunday or, if the church followed the liturgical calendar of the Quartodecimans, on any day of the week in spring when it was full moon.

The New Testament offers no explicit information as to whether the apostles celebrated yearly the Christian feast of Easter. Nevertheless, if we consider the solemn declaration of 1 Corinthians 5:7b-8 that "Christ our Passover has been sacrificed, let us celebrate the feast," we can at least conclude that the apostolic church attributed to the Jewish feast of Passover a Christian meaning. But did the apostles celebrate Christ's own passover as a liturgical feast? Acts 20:16 recounts that St. Paul decided to pass wide of Ephesus, as he was anxious to be in Jerusalem for the feast of Pentecost. Is there a suggestion here that the apostolic community commemorated the Christian events on the occasion of the Jewish feasts? If so, the yearly cycle, like the weekly, would form part of what art. 106 of the constitution regards as "a tradition handed down from the apostles."

Proponents of the Quartodeciman observance, like Polycarp of Smyrna and Polycrates of Ephesus, were adamant in their belief that their tradition of celebrating Easter at the full moon of spring had been handed down to them by no less than the apostles themselves. Those who observed Easter only on Sunday were equally convinced that their tradition came from the two apostles of Rome. It is not our purpose here to enter into the merit of the claims made by these two groups. What interests us is the conclusion that as far back as the end of the first century the practice of celebrating a yearly Easter was being attributed to the apostles themselves. However, A. Adam is of the opinion that "the paschal mystery of Christ was initially celebrated on Sunday as a weekly Pasch, until the feast of Easter was established as a yearly Pasch." The feast of Easter, according to him, "was introduced at the latest around the end of the first and the beginning of the second century."[17] Likewise, P. Jounel, basing himself on M. Richard's study, affirms that "it was not until the early years of the second century that there was any thought of celebrating a specifically Christian feast of Easter, and even then the Church of Rome waited until the second half of the first century before accepting it."[18]

There is, of course, no hard evidence that the yearly Easter celebration is of apostolic origin, though the early church Fathers mentioned above nurtured such a conviction. Nonetheless, the question can be approached from another angle. How did the apostolic church celebrate concretely a liturgical feast like Sunday? Acts 20:7 tells us that "on the first day of the week when we gathered for the breaking of bread, Paul preached" to the disciples at Troas.[19] Authors, like W. Rordorf, see in this text the existence of a regular Sunday liturgical assembly with the eucharist as the central celebration.[20] Today the typical celebration of a liturgical feast would include the eucharist and the liturgy of the hours equipped with related biblical and euchological texts. The *General Norms for the Liturgical Year and the Calendar* explains that "each day is made holy through the liturgical celebration of the people of God, especially through the eucharistic sacrifice and the divine office."[21]

If we expect to find in the New Testament these forms of celebrating Easter, we are courting great disappointment. But the point we are pressing is that the Christian celebration of Easter as a liturgical feast did not have to include initially the Lord's supper, except on Sunday. There is ample evidence that the first disciples of Jesus observed Passover, Unleavened Bread, and Pentecost. 1 Corinthians 5:7b-8, Acts 20:16, and Acts 20:6 are some of the respective texts that offer clear reference to Christian participation in Jewish feasts. The dynamic of inculturation at this early part of liturgical history would not have required anything more than a reintepretation of these feasts in the light of the saving work of Christ. Inculturation does not necessarily involve a change in existing ritual patterns and elements of the feast. What it requires is a change of perspective, a new manner of understanding the meaning of the feast. This is what St. Paul's classic text, "Christ our Passover has been sacrificed, let us celebrate the feast," seems to tell us. Surely every year when the disciples celebrated Passover according to the Jewish ritual, they recalled the blood not of the lambs of exodus but "of the new and everlasting covenant." After the pentecostal experience they would not have been able to celebrate the other Pentecosts without remembering the event and thanking God for the outpouring of the Holy Spirit upon the Christian community.

But apart from this consideration it does not seem liturgically accurate to focus the entire liturgical year on Sunday. The preferential treatment given to Sunday by art. 106 of the Constitution on the Liturgy has in fact created a lopsided liturgical year. Fortunately, the preceding art. 102 has already forestalled the imbalance by speaking of "the cycle of a year" in which the church unfolds the whole mystery of Christ from the moment of the incarnation to the day of Pentecost. Furthermore, the same article even sets Sunday and Easter side by side as two forms of celebrating Christ's paschal mystery: "Every week, on the day which the church has called the Lord's Day, it keeps the memory of the Lord's resurrection, which it also celebrates once a year, together with his blessed passion, in the most solemn festival of Easter."

If we read art. 102 in the light of its first draft where the Easter Vigil was given preeminence in the liturgical calendar, we can at the very least deduce that this article of the constitution considers Sunday and Easter as the two pivotal points of the liturgical year. Each in the framework of its own cycle celebrates the resurrection of Christ. The adverb "also" (*etiam* in the Latin original), which has a conjunctive force equivalent to "and," seems to indicate that both the weekly and the yearly cycles not only possess equal importance in the design of the liturgical calendar, but also run parallel to each other. Sunday is a weekly commemoration, while Easter is a yearly celebration. Sunday centers on the resurrection, while Easter embraces both the passion and the resurrection. The postconciliar thinking that Sunday is to the weekly what Easter is to the yearly cycle is perhaps not without foundation in art. 102 of the constitution, though alas art. 106 would have us think differently.

The problem of imbalance caused by art. 106 was addressed and fittingly solved by the *General Norms for the Liturgical Year and the Calendar*. Article 4 of this document, following the Constitution on the Liturgy, continues to call Sunday the Lord's Day in which the paschal mystery is celebrated. It upholds the apostolicity of Sunday observance, its origin in the resurrection of Christ, and its rank in the calendar as the original feastday. However, unlike the Constitution which employs the patristic expression "eighth day," this document prefers to call Sunday with the New Testament appellation "first day of the week." But what is truly remarkable about this postconciliar document is that it has boldly abandoned the idea of Sunday as the foundation and core of the whole liturgical year. Instead it decisively names the Easter triduum as "the culmination of the entire liturgical year." Thus it shifted the focus from Sunday to Easter. Its conclusion, which is marked by skillful use of the art of compromise, is a clever solution to the problem of a lopsided liturgical year: "The solemnity of Easter has the same kind of preeminence in the liturgical year that Sunday has in the week."[22]

The Jewish Antecedents of Easter

The Christian feast of Easter traces its origin to that "hour" when Christ made his own passover "from this world to the Father" (Jn 13:1). Since Christ came to his "hour" when the Jewish nation was celebrating the feast of Passover, the church reckons the date of Easter, taking into consideration the date of the Jewish Passover. Hence, to understand the theological and spiritual implications of the Easter date it would be helpful to review briefly the history of the Jewish Passover, particularly in respect to its cosmic elements.[23]

The ancient code of Leviticus 23:5-8 neatly distinguishes the feasts of Passover and Unleavened Bread: "The Passover of the Lord falls on the fourteenth day of the first month, at the evening twilight. The fifteenth day of this month is the Lord's feast of Unleavened Bread." Exodus 12 which treats them under two headings, namely verses 3-14 for Passover and verses 15-20 for Unleavened Bread, gives at least a clear impression of two distinct feasts. Deuteronomy 16:1-8, on the other hand, combines the two feasts and prescribes that for seven days the Passover sacrifice should be eaten only with unleavened bread.

From these and similar passages authors generally conclude that what was celebrated in later times as one feast lasting for seven days must have had separate origins. According to this theory, Passover was a pastoral rite held by nomads once a year in spring, while Unleavend Bread was an agricultural rite performed, also in spring, by Canaanite farmers. After the exodus the incoming nomads, who began to settle down as farmers, at first adopted the agricultural feast of Palestine and eventually annexed it to their own. Josuha 5:10-11 witnesses to this development: "While the Israelites were encamped at Gilgal on the plains of Jericho, they celebrated the Passover on the evening of the fourteenth of the month. On the day after the Passover they ate of the produce of the land in the form of unleavened cakes and parched grain."

J. Segal reverses this theory. He suggests that the two festivals were originally one, Passover being the opening and principal ceremony of a week-long celebration. He does away with the view that the Israelites were merely nomadic and did not till the earth until after they entered Canaan. "The Hebrew patriarchs," he points out, "were not nomads like the cattle-breeders of the Arabian deserts, but semi-nomads." Hence, "it is not that the two festivals have been merged to form a single festival; but a single feast has been divided into two in the Bible narrative, because only one group of ceremonies, the Pesah, appeared to have full relevance to the circumstances of the Exodus."[24] J. Segal may have a point about the early Hebrews as being a half-farmer, half-shepherd people. But it cannot be denied that the meaning and ritual elements of these two feasts differ quite radically. That is why they could not have been instituted from the beginning as a single feast.

Unleavened Bread suggests an agricultural festival at the ingathering of barley in spring. Since it was not possible to predict from year to year the exact time of harvest, this spring feast which lasted for seven days did not originally have a fixed date. The pre-Israelitic form of the celebration must have consisted in the ritual offering of the first sheaf of barley stalks to the agricultural deity. For the farm-settled people of Northern Palestine who worshiped in sanctuaries the rite of offering would have included a pilgrimage to these places. This particular character of the feast seems to have largely contributed to the evolution of Passover in the time of Ezechiel as a feast involving a yearly pilgrimage to the temple in Jerusalem. The prescriptions of Ezekiel 45:18-24, whereby the prophet enforced his centralizing reform, have transformed Passover from a local observance into a national festival whose center was the holy city. In a sense its original domestic character was sacrificed for the sake of unity.

To stress the feature of the feast as a new harvest, the Canaanite farmers ate only unleavened bread for seven days. Nothing of the preceding harvest must be mixed with the new. The tradition was religiously kept by the incoming Israelites who, as they began to settle down, readily adopted the native feast. Deuteronomy 16:4

commanded them that "nothing leavened may be found in all your territory for seven days." The Arab Beduins also ate unleavened bread, but because it was their normal daily bread, they attached no special cultic meaning to it. But for the Canaanite farmers it was unusual to eat unleavened bread. For them it had something to do with a religious rite and it had a symbolic meaning. The bread baked without yeast signified the turning point of the year, a new beginning of the agricultural cycle. It thus became a symbol and an experience of what M. Eliade would call "cosmic rebirth."[25] Every year creation renews itself during spring. The farmers who celebrated this cosmic rebirth expressed their participation in it through the unleavened bread of the new harvest, the symbol of a renewed creation ushered in every year by the season of spring.

In contrast to the feast of Unleavened Bread which the farmers kept for seven days in their sanctuaries, the feast of Passover was held by shepherds in their tents on the full moon of spring. Passover was the spring festival of nomadic shepherds during which they offered the firstlings of their flock as a kind of pastoral lambing sacrifice. As the more widely accepted etymology of *Pesah* (to skip or pass over, to spare) seems to indicate, it was originally celebrated by nomads as an apotropaeic or protective measure against the incursions of destructive cosmic powers that threatened the lives of both shepherds and flock. To chase away these unfriendly forces of nature they marked the lintels of their tents with the blood of the lamb.

The nature and activities of these cosmic powers are lost in the thick mists of the past. We can only surmise the terror they must have sown among the shepherds, exposed as they were to the changes of the seasons. Exodus 12:13 and 23 has preserved for us some vestiges of the "destroyer" who, as a personified agent of Yahweh, skipped over the blood-stained doors of the Israelites in Egypt, but struck down all the firstborn of the Egyptians. Perhaps this obscure figure, whose activities were directed against firstborn, claimed certain rights over them, in the same way as Yahweh, according to Exodus 13:1-2, claims as his inalienable property every firstborn of people and beast alike.

The Passover rite was celebrated in spring, the season when the nomads left their winter station in search of a greener and more abundant pasture. For the wandering shepherds it was a turning point of the year and a critical moment, a time laden with uncertainty. Migration brought with it the anxiety of encountering hostile cosmic forces along the way. The night before their departure, when the moon was full, the shepherds performed the apotropaeic rite in order to ensure a safe journey. The element of the full moon could have been, at least originally, a matter of convenience. The most suitable time to celebrate a nocturnal feast is obviously when it is bright. However, it would not be far-fetched to trace this element to some primitive moon cult that ascribed the growth and increase of plants and animals to the action of the moon.[26] But even if we dissociate the influence of the moon cult from the feast of Passover in its pre-exodus phase, we should perhaps not altogether ignore the symbolism of the full moon. For it signified what the ancient people expected to reap from their work: abundance and fullness of life.

On the eve of their historic departure from Egypt the Israelites performed the ancient rite of the shepherds in order to appeal to Yahweh for protection. Pharaoh had refused to let the Israelites sacrifice in the desert the firstlings of their herd, and so Yahweh decided to inflict vengeance on him and his land. Exodus 12:12 has recorded for us the ominous words of an angered God: "On this night I will go through Egypt, striking down every firstborn of the land, both man and beast, and executing judgment on all the gods of Egypt—I, the Lord!" The lamb was slaughtered, the lintel and the two doorposts of the houses of the Israelites were sprinkled with its blood, and as Exodus 12:29 recounts, "at midnight the Lord slew every firstborn in the land of Egypt, from the firstborn of Pharaoh on the throne to the firstborn of the prisoner in the dungeon, as well as all the firstborn of the animals."

The event of the Passover night solemnly inaugurated the exodus, that dramatic and marvellous act of Yahweh in favor of his people. Henceforth the spring rite of Passover would be associated with the exodus itself, it would become part of Israel's history of salvation, it would be historicized. What had been originally a yearly festival of migrating shepherds was transformed into a yearly memorial of Israel's exodus toward the promised land. Thus Exodus 12:26-27 directs that "when your children ask you, What does this rite of yours mean?, you shall reply, This is the Passover sacrifice of the Lord, who passed over the houses of the Israelites in Egypt; when he struck down the Egyptians, he spared our houses."

In the process of historization the cosmic elements of the Passover feast were not lost, though they were subsequently reinterpreted in the light of what took place on the night of the exodus. The mysterious cosmic forces which in the past had been a menace to the safety of the nomads and their flock came to be understood, especially in rabbinic literature, as the avenging angel of Yahweh.[27] The feast continued to be held at the full moon of the spring equinox, because it was at this point in time when the season of freedom from slavery commenced for the people of Israel. In the words of Exodus 12:42, "this was a night of vigil for the Lord, as he led them out of the land of Egypt; so on this same night all the Israelites must keep a vigil for the Lord throughout their generations." Thus what was formerly the nomads' vigil for the protection of their god was regarded by the Israelites as a vigil in honor of Yahweh who led them safely out of Egypt "with a mighty hand." Likewise, the other elements of the ancient festival were inserted into the framework of God's saving intervention. Thus Exodus 12:11 instructs the fleeing Israelites to eat the roasted lamb hastily with girdle around their waist, sandals on their feet, and staff in their hand.[28]

After the feast of Unleavened Bread had been absorbed by the feast of Passover, it too became part of the event of exodus. It too underwent the process of historization. Exodus 12:33-34 narrates that the Egyptians, tormented by endless plagues inflicted on them by Yahweh, finally realized that the only way to avert a greater calamnity was to send the Israelites away. They urged them to hurry up and leave Egypt. And so the Israelites "took their dough before it was leavened, in their kneading bowls wrapped around their cloaks on their shoulders." Deuteronomy 16:3 calls the unleavened bread "bread of emergency" and prescribes that for seven days the paschal lamb be eaten only with it, "that you may remember as long as you live the day of your departure from the land of Egypt; for in frightened haste you left the land of Egypt."

A Sacramental View of Nature

The church has always been attentive to the relation of the Easter date to cosmic elements such as spring, spring equinox, and full moon. These cosmic elements have, in the course of time, greatly influenced the theological thinking on Easter as well as the shape of the liturgical celebration. We still observe them when we reckon from year to year the date of Easter, but do they retain the importance, if not the mystique, they once possessed? And what symbolic relevance do they have in those regions of the world where Easter is celebrated in summer or fall?

It is not rare to meet people who find it rather curious that a spiritual feast like Easter should continue to be dependent on the world of nature for its calendar and, to a large extent, its theme and symbols. There are also people who claim that, notwithstanding the growth in environmental and ecological awareness, modern people's attitude toward nature is generally quite devoid of any religious and symbolic underpinning. And even granting that for many spring still possesses its charm, the full moon its romance, and the night its mystery, the sacramental vision of nature that characterized the patristic times has been dimmed by modern science and often eclipsed by an entirely materialistic consideration of natural resources.

But for the ancient world nature was the locus of divine interventions and of human encounter with God. Nature and time were not only signs of God's dealings with people; they were symbols that embodied, manifested, and brought along his salvation. In short, they enjoyed a sacramental quality and played a sacramental role. This is the theology upon which the early church's understanding and celebration of Easter were firmly built. It will not be an easy task for anyone who is indifferent to nature to work through the patristic literature on Easter. This is not to say that the church associated the feast of Easter with some natural festival to welcome the advent of spring. The focal point of the feast has always been the paschal sacrifice and resurrection of Christ. Yet the world of nature and the times and seasons of the year are the locus where these divine mysteries took place and where we encounter them. Perhaps the church's attention to the cosmic elements of Easter has after all a clear and full message to the people of today.

NOTES

1. S. Marsili, "La teologia della liturgia nel Vaticano II," in *Anamnesis*, vol. 1 (Turin 1974) 98. The English translation is mine.

2. Ibid.

3. English text in *Documents on the Liturgy* (Collegeville 1982) 1158. Henceforth, *DOL*.

4. Ambrose of Milan, *Letter 23*, 12-13 (PL 16:1030).

5. Augustine of Hippo, *Letter 55*, 24 (PL 33:215).

6. See A. Nocent, "Il triduo pasquale e la settimana santa," *in Anamnesis*, vol. 6 (Genoa 1988) 97-115; P. Jounel, "The Easter Triduum," in *The Church at Prayer*, vol. 4 (Collegeville 1986) 46-56; T. Talley, *The Origins of the Liturgical Year* (New York 1986) 13-67.

7. Jounel, "The Easter Vigil" 35.

8. Ibid. 39.

9. Nocent, "Il triduo pasquale" 99-100.

10. Theophilus of Alexandria, *Prologue to Festal Letters* (PG 65:48A).

11. See P. Jounel, "Déclaration du II Concile du Vatican sur la révision du calendrier," *La Maison-Dieu* 77 (1964) 219-221; A. Adam, *The Liturgical Year* (New York 1981) 59-62.

12. Text in *DOL* 27.

13. *Acta et Documenta Concilio Oecumenico Vaticano II Apparando,* Series II (Praeparatoria) vol. 3 (Vatican City 1969) 55.

14. S. Marsili, *Teologia liturgica. Anno liturgico* (Rome 1977, pro manuscripto) 36.

15. *Schema Constitutionis de Sacra Liturgia,* Emendationes IX, De Anno Liturgico (Vatican City 1963) 17. For a fuller treatment of this question see, A. Chupungco, "The Place of Sunday in the Liturgical Year: A Rereading of SC 106," *Ecclesia Orans* 1 (1984) 133-151.

16. J. Jungmann, "The Weekly Cycle in the Liturgy," *Pastoral Liturgy* (London 1962) 251-254.

17. A. Adam, *The Liturgical Year* 24; J. Van Goudoever, *Biblical Calendars* (Leiden 1961) 164-175.

18. J. Jounel, "The Easter Cycle," in *The Church at Prayer,* vol. 4 (Collegeville 1985) 33; see M. Richard, "La question pascale au II. siècle," *L'Orient syrien* 6 (1961) 179-212.

19. See M. Rooney, "La domenica," in *Anamnesis,* vol. 6 (Genoa 1988) 71-74.

20. W. Rordorf, *Der Sonntag. Geschichte des Ruhe-und Gottesdiensttages im ältesten Christentum* (Zurich 1962) 193-202; Rordorf, "Domenica," *Dizionario Patristico e di Antichità Christiane,* vol. 1 (Casale Monferrato 1983) 1010-1011.

21. Art. 3, *DOL* 1156.

22. Art. 18, *DOL* 1158.

23. R. de Vaux, *Ancient Israel, Its Life and Institutions* (New York 1961); I. Elbogen, *Der jüdische Gottesdienst in seiner geschichtlichen Entwicklung* (Hildesheim 1962); H.-J. Kraus, *Gottesdienst in Israel* (Munich 1962); H. Haag, *Vom alten zum neuen Pascha* (Stuttgart 1971); Haag, "Pâque," *Dictionnaire de la Bible,* Supplément, vol. 6 (Paris 1960) 1120-1149; T. Chary, "Pâques, mystère de salut permanent," *Lectio Divina* 112 (Paris 1982) 19-31; H. Auf der Maur, "Die jährliche Osterfeier," *Gottesdienst der Kirche* 5 (Regensburg 1983) 56-63; A. Saldarini, *Jesus and Passover* (New York 1984) 5-15; E. Otto, "Pesah," *Theologisches Wörterbuch zum Alten Testament,* vol. 6 (Stuttgart 1989) 659-676; G. Yee, *Jewish Feasts and the Gospel of John* (Wilmington 1989).

24. J. Segal: *The Hebrew Passover from the Earliest Times to A.D. 70* (London 1963) 93-175.

25. M. Eliade, *Cosmos and History* (New York 1959) 68.

26. See M. Eliade, *The Sacred and the Profane* (New York 1955) 68-70.

27. *Pesachim, Die Mischna* 3. Traktat (Giessen 1912) 195.

28. See Philo of Alexandria, *On Special Laws II*, Loeb Classical Library, vol. 7 (Cambridge 1958) 158; Josephus, *Jewish Antiquities*, vol. 2 (London 1961) 317.

Chapter Two
Easter and the Season of Spring

Spring in Jewish Tradition

IN ANCIENT RELIGIONS WHERE COSMOGONY OR THE ORIGIN OF THE UNIVERSE WAS the centerpiece of a people's worldview, the start of the calendar year coincided with the mythical first day of creation. In his classic work *The Sacred and the Profane* M. Eliade tells us that "at each New Year the cosmogony is reiterated, the world is re-created, and to do this is also to create time—that is, to regenerate it by beginning it anew."[1] For Israel, however, whose religion is rooted in historical events or historicized rites, time does not flow in an endless cyclic course. It is linear, which means that it moves from one stage or moment to the next. These stages are the time before creation, the historical time marked by divine manifestations to Israel, and the Day of the Lord at the "last times."[2] Hence, in Jewish theology the New Year festival does not repeat the primordial moment of creation; it does not involve a resumption of the cosmogonic time when the universe passed from chaos to cosmos.

Nevertheless, every New Year the people of Israel held before their eyes the wonder of God's creation. And as they admired and blessed God for his work, they experienced in some mysterious way the recurrence of the cosmogonic time, which the New Year celebration aimed to recapture and transport to the present. Cosmogony became, as it were, a contemporary event which they could witness with their own eyes, in the same way as the exodus became an actual event in which they must take part through the yearly celebration of the paschal meal. The celebration of the New Year meant that cosmogony, which took place outside the realm of historical time, broke into time and became part of Israel's history of salvation. In biblical theology creation and salvation interlock. This is why the exodus is considered a second creation.

New Year was held by different peoples at different times of the year. The diversity depended largely on the kind of lunar calendar the people used. Ancient Egypt kept New Year sometime in the middle of July. But New Year at springtime was a more widespread tradition. At least since the time of King Hammurabi (c. 1800 B.C.) Babylon kept New Year or the *Akitu* in spring. It was a twelve-day festival commemorating the victory of the god-king Marduk over the goddess Tiamat whose body he split in two to form heaven and earth. The creation epic *Enuma Elish* was recited over and over again in the temple of Marduk in an effort to recapture the mythical story of creation: "When on high the heaven had not been named, firm ground below had not been called by name . . ."[3] A mimetic combat between Marduk and Tiamat was staged in order to render the cosmogonic story narrated by the epic poem present through anamnesis.[4] The Persians also kept New Year in spring when they held the six-day festival called *Nawroz*. The celebration expressed their belief that just as the universe was created in spring, so the entire cosmos was renewed yearly in spring: "This is a new day of a month of a new year; all that time has worn out must be renewed!"[5]

In Israel, before the exile, the calendar year began in autumn, in the month of Tishri (September-October) which is the first month of the civil year and the seventh of the liturgical year.[6] Before the exile the New Year festival, called *Rosh ha-shana*, was observed on the tenth of Tishri which was the day of the autumnal equinox.[7] This means that in the pre-exilic calendar there was a balance between the two equal sections of the year. The first month or Abib (called Nisan after the exile) balanced with the seventh month or Tishri; the spring equinox with the autumnal equinox; and the tenth of Abib, when the paschal lambs for immolation were separated from the herd, with the tenth of Tishri, when the new calendar year commenced. During the exile and thereafter the New Year day was moved to the first day of Tishri to give way to a new feast, the Day of Atonement or *Yom Kippur*, which was to be held, according to Leviticus 23:27, on the tenth. Leviticus 23:24 witnesses to this post-exilic calendar revision: "On the first day of the seventh month you shall keep a sabbath rest, with a sacred assembly and with trumpet blasts as a reminder."

Around the year 100 A.D. the observance of New Year on the first day of Tishri was an accepted fact in the Mishnah and other rabbinic writings. The tractate *Rosh ha-shana*, however, speaks not of one but of four New Year days in the calendar: "There are four New Year days: on the first of Nisan is the New Year for kings and feasts; on the first of Elul is the New Year for the tithe of cattle; on the first of Tishri is the New Year for the years, for the year of Release and Jubilee, for the plants and for vegetables; on the first of Shebat is the New Year for trees."[8] We gather from this that in the first-century Israel the civil New Year, which *Rosh ha-shana* calls the New Year for the years, began on the first day of Tishri. Throughout the rest of the tractate this alone is referred to as the New Year, the "day for the blowing of trumpets" (Lv 23:24; Nm 29:1).

But in biblical tradition the first day of Nisan is also considered a New Year day, thanks to the influence of the Babylonian calendar and the prescription of Exodus 12:2 which ordains that "this month shall stand at the head of your calendar; you shall reckon it the first month of the year." *Rosh ha-shana*, as we have seen, regards it as rather the beginning of the liturgical year which opens with the feast of Passover: it is the New Year for feasts. Philo of Alexandria, who was familiar with the tradition of his people, recognizes the distinction between the civil calendar which began in the month of Tishri and the liturgical calendar which began in Nisan. He agrees that in reality the month of Nisan "comes seventh in order and number as judged by the cycle of the sun." Nonetheless, "in importance it is first, and therefore is described as first in sacred books."[9] For him the month of Nisan obviously derives its importance from the celebration of the feast of Passover.

In Judaism, as in other religions in the ancient near east, the day of the New Year was associated with cosmogony. The question was, which New Year, considering that there were four of them. The following early second-century debate is a typical example of how the learned deliberated on such issues. According to Rabbi Eliezer ben Hyrkanos, "the world was created in Tishri; the first parents were formed in Tishri and they died in Tishri . . . How do we know that the universe was created in the month of Tishri? It is written, And God said: let earth bring forth vegetation, seed-bearing plants and fruit trees. Tishri is the month when the earth is fully green, and trees abound with fruit." Rabbi Joshua ben Kanania held the contrary opinion. He claimed that "the world was created in Nisan; the first parents were formed in Nisan and they died in Nisan . . . How do we know that the universe was created in the month of Nisan? It is written, The earth brought forth vegetation, seed-bearing plants of different kinds and trees that bear fruit. Nisan is the month when the earth brings forth vegetation and the trees bear fruit."[10]

People might dismiss this method of argumentation as a rather naive attempt to prove a point through use of biblical passages. We should note that the writings of several church Fathers and even of great scholastic theologians were not exempt from such a method. But apart from this seeming naiveté, there is probably more theological depth in what is said than meets the eye. While it is quite obvious that the foregoing rabbinic opinions used Scripture merely to pad out an argument regardless of correct biblical interpretation, it would not be fair to say that they have not contributed to a better understanding of salvation history. The rabbis assigned in a particular season of the year the principal events of salvation history: the creation of the world, the creation and death of the first parents, and the activities of the Hebrew patriarchs. It would appear at first sight that their aim for doing this was to heighten the importance of the months of Tishri or Nisan. In reality, it would be more accurate to say that what they accomplished in effect was to show the connection between these events as various phases of one history of salvation. Viewed from this perspective, the issue on whether cosmogony actually took place in autumn or spring becomes moot. Still it is important to note that the latter tradition had a considerable influence on the early patristic literature on Easter.

The *Babylonian Talmud on Berakot* supports the theory of cosmogony in spring with arguments from astronomy. Of the background of this work we possess only fragmentary information. The text is obscure, indeed enigmatic, but the little we are able to gather from its analysis can be rewarding. The text reads:

> The learned ones teach: those who see the sun at its turning point, the moon at its brightest phase, the stars on their paths, and the constellations in array should say, Praised be the One who brought creation to its perfection! When does it happen? Abbaye answers: Every twenty-eight years, when the cycle starts anew, and the turning point of the month of Nisan falls in Saturn, on the night between Tuesday and Wednesday.[11]

Abbaye (c. 338 A.D.) seems to base his observation on a cycle of twenty-eight years, when the earth and Saturn are on a synodic period, and during spring, when both planets traverse the zodiac sign of Aries or Taurus. Ancient astronomers did much speculation on the recurrence of such celestial cycles. The cycle of twenty-eight years, often called the *circulus solis* in contrast to the yearly cycle or *anni circulus*, was well known in antiquity. It is the result of multiplying seven and four. Seven stands for the number of years it would take so that the first day of the year would fall again on the same day of the week. Four stands for the leap year. Abbaye's preference for this cycle could have been greatly influenced by an ancient theory according to which Saturn made a complete revolution around the earth every twenty-eight years. The myth of the Saturnian "golden age" further corroborated the belief that the universe was created in the state of perfection and splendor, and that these qualities could still be observed during the month of Nisan every twenty-eight years.

The turning point of Nisan referred to by Abbaye is the middle of the month or the night of the full moon between the fourteenth and the fifteenth, when the Passover meal was eaten. Abbaye makes an amazingly exact reckoning of the night when all this was to happen, the night between Tuesday and Wednesday. In the cycle of twenty-eight years the first day of the year should, theoretically, fall every year on the same day of the week. In the "ideal calendar" of the *Book of Jubilees* the fourteenth-fifteenth day of the first, fourth, seventh, and tenth month always fell on Tuesday-Wednesday, so that the date of Passover was tied down to a fixed day of the week.[12]

The Christian tradition of cosmogony in spring is the direct legacy of Philo of Alexandria's work which carries the title *Special Laws*. His reflections on the subject are contained in chapters 27, 28, and 29 of the second book. In an irrevocable way they have shaped the patristic thinking on the date of Easter, especially with respect to the allegorical and spiritual interpretation of its cosmic elements.

According to Philo, God created the world in springtime, in the month of Nisan. This month comes "seventh in order and number as judged by the cycle of the sun, but in importance it is first, and therefore is described as first in the sacred book."[13] Nisan derives its importance partly from exodus and partly from the fact that it was the month when God created the world. As Philo puts it, "every year God reminds us of the creation of the world by setting before our eyes the season of spring when everything blooms and flowers." In line with the rabbinic tradition of the Babylonian Talmud, he supports his statement with arguments based on verse 12 of Genesis 1: "The earth brought forth every kind of plant that bears seed and every kind of fruit tree on earth that bears fruit with its seed in it."

At which particular part of spring did God create the world? Philo answers that at the time of cosmogony "the elements were separated and placed in harmonious order with reference to themselves and each other." The distinguishing traits of the equinox in the account of Genesis 1 were the equal division of the elements of light and darkness and land and water, as well as the resulting equilibrium between them. And so, in accord with the ancient belief that the universe was created in order, harmony, and splendor, Philo writes: "In spring equinox we have a likeness and portraiture of that first epoch in which this world was created," or in other words, God created the world at that precise moment in cosmogonic time, which we know today as the spring equinox.

Spring is the likeness and portraiture of cosmogony, or as Philo says early on, it is "the image of the primal origin reproduced from it like the imprint from an archetypal seal."[14] Born and raised in an historical religion, he rejects the pagan myth of eternal return. In spring pagans held New Year festivals whose basic content was the symbolic repetition of cosmogony through ritual ceremonies, such as extinguishing the old fires, fertility rites, and purifications. Through orgies and mimetic combats they symbolized the abolition of all existing social and moral order. They made an attempt to reduce time and cosmos to the primordial chaos in order to repeat the eternally recurring passage from chaos to cosmos.[15] This explains why the days during which the festival was held were often considered to be outside the normal calendar days. A fourth-century writer, Q.J. Hilarian, reports the practice of setting aside five days outside the regular calendar "in remembrance of God's creation."[16] According to Philo, who must have regarded all this with disdain, spring is not a repetition but an imitation and portrayal of the first day of creation. His use of the words *trópos* and *sphragís* would seem to suggest that he viewed spring as the bearer and seal of the cosmogonic act.

Lastly, the feast of Passover is celebrated in springtime because of its highly evocative quality. This season brings to mind everything that Passover signifies: creation, new birth, renewal of life. The traits of springtime enable Passover to depict in a graphic way the event of the exodus, the creation of Israel as God's chosen people, and allegorically "the passage of souls from vices to virtue."[17] That the feast of Passover is held when it is full moon and the whole of creation proudly displays all its natural beauty and splendor can only mean, according to Philo, that a new life has begun for the people of Israel. Thus the relation of spring to Passover rests not only on historical fact but on symbolism and allegory as well. For Philo and the early Christian writers, symbols render the historical fact present and actual.

Spring in Christian Tradition

The association of spring with the Christian feast of Easter surfaced for the first time in Origen's *Commentary on Song of Songs*. Unlike later writers who also borrowed from Philo of Alexandria, he does not connect spring with cosmogony. What he sees in spring or the passing of winter is the time of Christ's passion. Commenting on Song of Songs 2:11 Origen writes: "Winter is past, the rains are over and gone. This passage indicates the time of Christ's passion. For he suffered after the season of winter and rains."[18] It might be useful to make the observation that in his typical manner of reading Scripture Origen does not refer here to the historical time of Christ's passion "after the season of winter and rains" but to the allegory provided by spring. Origen interprets the end of winter rains and the coming of spring to mean that Christ's suffering took place after John the Baptist, the last of the prophets, had been beheaded. For the prophets, explains Origen, were like the rains sent by God to water the earth with his word. At the coming of springtime, which is Christ's paschal mystery, their role in God's plan of salvation ceased.

But spring pervaded Easter theology and celebration only in the full flood of Philo's allegorism and spirituality. With little or no restraint a good number of the Fathers who came after Origen adopted the approach of Philo. The result of this was the emergence of a Christian reflection on the feast of Easter in which the principal characters were spring, creation, and salvation.[19]

One of the first to use the insights of Philo to great advantage was Eusebius of Caesarea. His explanation why Easter is kept in spring and not in the other seasons of the year reflects the influence of the Jew whom he did not hesitate to call a Christian. In his treatise on *The Feast of Easter* he reasoned that in winter nature is melancholic, in summer it is burnt by the heat of the sun, while in autumn it is bereft and despoiled of its fruit. Spring alone can offer to the feast of Easter a truly suitable setting. To the dignity of the feast correspond the grace and beauty of the season. Carried away by his contemplation of springtime, Eusebius exults in its advent:

> In spring the sun begins to run on its first course, while the moon transforms the night into a bright day. Spring dispels the dreadful winter storms, shortens the long hours of the night, and controls the floods. And now with new and resplendent calm the sea is made tranquil for sailors, and the climate mild for travellers on land. The plants are rich with seed and the trees are laden with fruit.[20]

Eusebius calls spring "the head of the entire year." By this he meant more than the numerical ordering of months in the calendar. Faithful to the tradition of Philo, he wanted to affirm that God created the world in springtime and that this season is consequently the image of cosmogony: "This is the season that conveys to us the time when the universe was created, the earth was formed, the lights were produced, and heaven and earth and all things in them were brought into being."[21] That is why, spring displays the same traits as those present when the world first came into existence: harmony, order, mildness, fruitfulness. It would seem that in the thinking of Eusebius springtime carries us back to the initial point whence time flowed, or at least it allows us to witness in its manifestations the wonderful work of God's creation.

But the chief concern of Eusebius as a Christian writer was to show the relation between spring and Christ's passover. Spring is the season not only of the first creation, but also of the second and more magnificent one. He points out that "it was at this season when the Savior of the whole universe celebrated the mystery of his own feast. The great light shone upon the world with the rays of religion and time seemed to envelop the birth of the universe."[22] When Christ accomplished the mystery of his death and resurrection, the world was created anew; it experienced the advent of a new spring. Brighter than the sun of the first spring, the risen Savior began to shed his light on the human race. Eusebius adds that at Christ's passover time itself (*kairós* in Greek) encompassed the birth of the universe. In patristic literature, as in other writings in antiquity, *kairós* often referred to sacred time, to a time filled with divine grace and salvation. In the tradition of Philo springtime is the *kairós* of creation and the exodus. Eusebius adopts this and draws the conclusion that when Christ rose from the dead the universe was enveloped in the *kairós* of divine blessing.[23]

The theme of creation and salvation in spring worked its way through several patristic writings. We meet it in Cyril of Jerusalem's catechetical lecture, *The Resurrection of Christ*, and Gregory of Nazianzus' homily on *The New Sunday*. To the query, "at what season did the Savior rise, in summer or at another time?" Cyril replies that it was in spring.

> Is not the land now full of flowers, and are not the vines being pruned? You see how he also said that the winter was past. For in this month Xanthicus spring is already come. This is the time, the first month among the Hebrews, in which the feast of the Passover is celebrated, formerly in figure, but now in truth. This is the season when the world was created. For God then said, Let the earth bring forth vegetation, yielding seed according to its kind and according to its likeness.[24]

Thus Cyril assigns the creation of the world and the resurrection of Christ both in spring, thereby intimating a certain unity and continuity between these two events.

Gregory of Nazianzus, on the other hand, speaks of spring as the most suitable among the seasons for celebrating the feast of Easter. His description of springtime depicts the image of nature adorning itself for a grand cosmic celebration.

> Everything contributes to the beauty and joy of the feast. The queen of the seasons prepares a feast for the queen of days, and presents to her all the beautiful and delightful things she possesses. The sky is transparent, the sun radiant, the moon brilliant, and the choir of stars bright. The springs of water are clear and the rivers full, for these are now freed from the fetters of ice. The fields emit sweet scents, green plants sprout, and lambs bound in green pastures.[25]

Gregory is ecstatic in his praises of spring, and who would not be after a severe winter? What comes across, however, is not so much the loveliness of the season as the exalted nature of the feast.

Patristic literature abounds in homilies, festal letters, and treatises which take delight in this theme. To examine all of them could be rather wearisome, because they often repeat the same things or seem merely to recite them from memory. But there are a number of treatises which stand out from the others for their original contribution to the subject.

One such work is the anonymous homily *On Easter* written in Greek toward the end of the fourth century.[26] Among the various topics addressed by the homilist we focus on the connection he sees between spring and the feast of Easter. To the question why spring or the month of Easter is the first month of the year he first gives an answer from the side of the Jews. He refers his listeners to "a tradition of the Hebrew people according to which it was in spring when God, the artisan and creator of all things, formed the universe."[27] Taking note of the natural harmony and order of the universe at this time of the year, he explains that for the Jews this signified the beginning of cosmogony and the coming of a new year. For them "the beauty of the world in spring reflects the first flowering of creation."

However, this type of reasoning does not particularly appeal to the anonymous homilist. Nisan, he affirms, is the first month of the year, not because it was the season of cosmogony, but because it was the month chosen by Christ for the celebration of his passion, "the spiritual feast of his passover." Furthermore, if on account of Christ's passover spring is the beginning of the calendar year, it is also on account of this mystery that spring is the "sovereign and head of all times and ages." For Christ who accomplished his saving work in spring is "the first-begotten and the firstborn of everything visible and invisible." Because Christ is the *protógonos* and *protótokos* of all creation, spring is the *kephalé* and *prote hegemonía* of every epoch of human history. Lastly, spring indicates the truth about Christ. God ordained that it should head the months of the year and all ages in order that it might be the symbol of Christ's own sovereignty.

The anonymous homilist's reflection on spring is exclusively centered on Christ's mystery, which he presents as the antitype or fulfillment of God's promise of salvation. He departs from the rabbinic tradition of spring cosmogony and confines the basis of his argument to Christ's mystery. This process of *christologization* is echoed by St. Gregory of Nazianzus who suggests that though Nisan was, from the start, the first month in the Hebrew calendar, "it became so later because of the mystery of Christ."[28]

The Latin world also explored the theme of cosmogony in spring. St. Ambrose of Milan, an ardent admirer of Philo, addresses the question in the first of nine Easter homilies which have reached us under the title of *Exameron*.[29] Commenting on the opening verse of Genesis 1, "In the beginning, when God created the heavens and the earth," he explains that the word "beginning" (*principium*) alludes to another beginning (*initium*) which is found in Exodus 12:2, namely "This month shall be for you the beginning of the year."[30] Both beginnings, one of the creation of the world, the other of the salvation of Israel, occurred in spring. Ambrose sees in this a continuity between the two acts of God: cosmogony led to the exodus, creation to salvation.

But what had been foreshadowed by these two events became a reality at the coming of Christ and continues to be so "when his passover is celebrated every year in spring." In the great tradition of Philo, Ambrose calls the Christian feast of Passover *transitus* or passage. Like Philo, he understands passover allegorically to mean "the passage of souls from vices to virtue, from the passions of the flesh to grace and sobriety of spirit, from the old leaven of evil and wickedness to truth and sincerity."[31] He applies this in a particular way to his neophytes: "To those who have been born anew Scripture says, This month shall be for you the beginning of months, it shall be for you the first of the months of the year."

The foregoing reflections are remarkably and succinctly summed up by a writer whom we only know as Pseudo-Ambrose: "Easter is called passage (*transitus*). This feast is thus called, because it was at that time when the children of Israel passed over from Egypt and the Son of God himself passed from this world to the Father."[32]

Ambrose claims that time began in the season of spring. God created the world "in the pleasant mildness of spring." He did not do it in winter or summer. These are not images of creation, because "tender plants cannot bear the hardship inflicted by the biting frost nor suffer the harm caused by the scorching heat." But Ambrose is not content with this type of argument drawn from natural observation. To press the point he invokes, in the manner of Philo and the rabbis, the authority of Exodus 12:1: "Scripture tells us that the world was created in spring when it says, This month is for you the beginning of months, it is the first month of the year. Scripture calls spring the first month." And ever since, spring has constantly manifested itself as the *mundi imago nascentis*, the image of a world which is reborn every year "at the same moment as when the Lord first said, Let the earth produce vegetation."[33]

We come across similar ideas in the *Paschal Tract on the Exodus* written by Gaudentius of Brescia toward the year 406. Although his chief aim in this work is to present Christ's resurrection as the antitype or fulfillment of the exodus, Gaudentius devotes part of it to the question of the Easter date. "The Lord Jesus," he affirms, "wanted that the feast of Easter should be held at the suitable time, that is, after the fog of autumn and desolation of winter and before the heat of summer" or, in short, in spring.[34] For Gaudentius the sun in spring is the symbol of Christ, the Sun of Justice. As the sun gently dispels the darkness of winter and melts the ice, so Christ, "by the tranquil light of his resurrection, scatters the darkness of the Jews and softens the hardness of the gentiles before the fire of the imminent judgment." By his resurrection Christ summons the entire creation back to its primordial state of peace and harmony which was thrown to confusion by the prince of darkness.

Gaudentius claims that March was the month decreed by God to be the beginning of the year. He claims too on the basis of "an ancient and venerable tradition" that Christ actually rose from the dead in the month of March, on Sunday, the day "when the world came into being." For Gaudentius this is not mere coincidence; it is all part of a divine plan. He sees a profound truth that lies buried in it. He explains:

> The Son of God, through whom all things were made, raised the fallen world by his resurrection on the same day as when he created it from nothing, in order that every being in heaven and on earth might be reformed in him.[35]

By rising from the dead at the moment of cosmogony Christ showed that the Creator of the world is also its Savior.

There are other Easter tracts that contain this doctrinal insight. The fourth-century Nicetas of Remesiana writes in his treatise *De Ratione Paschae*:

> Creation, which had been subjected to slavery when the world was made, was freed by Christ through his passion. That is why his suffering coincided with the time when creation was held in slavery.[36]

Pope Leo the Great repeats this in an *Homily on the Passion*:

> The holy month of spring shines forth because of the celebration of the feast announced by all the other feasts; as the world began in spring, so the Christian people have their origin also in spring.[37]

In passing we note that this doctrine, which affirms that the Creator of the world is at the same time its Savior, had an impact also on the practical question of how to reckon the date of Easter. Its implication was that the feast of Christ's passover could not be held outside the time frame of spring. The spurious *Acta Synodi Caesariensis* reports that at the synod held in Caesarea in Palestine in the year 334 the bishops decided at the outset that "we must first inquire when the world was created, and when this shall have been diligently studied, then we can establish correctly the canon on Easter date."[38]

We meet similar reflections on spring cosmogony and salvation in a little work written in Latin by a certain Apponius.[39] This author probably lived in Syria toward the end of the fourth century or, according to another opinion, in the first half of the fifth century. In his work, which carries the title *In Canticum Canticorum Expositio*, he relates spring to the various stages of salvation history beginning with cosmogony and culminating in the establishment of the church. He notes how "at the coming of springtime, the precursor of summer, winter is put to flight and every creature rejoices at its own renewal." He observes how animals construct dens, birds build their nest, and reptiles feast on earth's bounty. In spring nature returns to life.

> In the same way, after the frightful winter of idolatry and the deception of sophistry, Christ our Lord adorned the earth with the flowers of the work of martyrs and all holy people through his passion, which is our true passage from death to life.[40]

According to Apponius, the passion of Christ is a new kind of spring analogous in its effects to cosmic spring. It is our spiritual spring, our *transitus* or passage from death to life. It has repelled the errors of false religion and of false philosophy. Winter is past, the rains are over and gone. A new spring now covers the face of the earth; it is the springtime of good works.

A remarkable trait of Apponius' treatise is how it associates spring with the principal events of salvation history from creation to the establishment of the church. We meet this practice also in Judaism, especially among the rabbis. It is not unlikely that Apponius, whose work strongly suggests rabbinic influence, was familiar with this tradition. Rabbi Joshua ben Kanania taught that the world was created in Nisan, the first parents were created in Nisan and died in Nisan, and the principal events in Hebrew history took place in

Nisan.[41] Among Christian writers an early example of this is the second-century *Homily on Easter* by Melito of Sardis which commemorates the creation of the world, exodus, promulgation of the law, and entry into the promised land.[42] In this sense, the celebration of Easter for both Israel and the Christians appears to be the compendium of the history of salvation.[43]

The following text from Apponius shows the various events with which spring is linked:

> In spring all creatures came into being and the first parent was formed from the clay of the earth. In spring Jacob was called from Mesopotamia to his own land. In spring the children of Israel were led out of the land of Egypt, the blood of the lamb which prefigured Christ turned the destroyer of Egypt away, and they entered the promised land after crossing the Jordan. In spring Christ our Redeemer, ascending by the example of his death from the valley of tears to the mountain of Paradise, summons the church, saying: Arise, hasten, my love, my lovely one, and come, for winter is past."[44]

In this text Apponius commemorates four moments in the history of salvation. The first is the creation of the world and the first parents. The second is the return of Jacob or Israel from Mesopotamia to represent thereby the election of the chosen people. The third is the exodus from Egypt, the crossing of the river Jordan, also referred to as the second exodus, and entry into Palestine. The fourth is Christ's passage from death (valley of tears) to new life (mountain of Paradise) and the call of the church. The *Book of Jubilees* assigns the return of Jacob to Palestine on 21 Nisan. It also recalls the other principal events which happened in Nisan, namely the sacrifice of Isaac, Abraham's arrival on Mount Sion, and Jacob's arrival at Bethel.[45]

Spring is the mirror of cosmogony, because it reflects the renewal or rebirth of creation. The Fathers of the church saw in this natural phenomenon a graphic illustration of what takes place when the springtime of Christ's passover is celebrated by the church. As spring brings rebirth and salvation to nature, so it also brings the feast of Easter to the church. Spring acquires, so to speak, a sacramental character. It becomes the bearer of God's presence and of his wonderful deed in Christ. This in so many words is what we read in the fifth-century *Festal Letters* written by Cyril of Alexandria.[46]

In his ninth festal letter Cyril writes: "Spring brings to us the resurrection of the Savior, by which he restored us to newness of life, after he had escaped the corruption of death."[47] Spring announces the presence of Christ's paschal mystery and hence of our spiritual rebirth. Year after year spring "reveals itself as the new season of our Savior's resurrection."[48] Viewed from this perspective, spring is *kairós*, that is, a sacred season in which we are privileged with a more profound experience of the presence of God and his work of salvation.

Spring is not only the presence but also the graphic description of what Christ did for us. Cyril develops this thought in his sixteenth festal letter: "The convenient time to celebrate Easter is spring, since besides other things it describes, as on a canvas, the great work of Christ."[49] He invites his readers to gaze upon "in the blessings of spring the work our Savior gloriously accomplished at his coming, and to contemplate the divine beauty that is portrayed by the realities that fall beneath our senses."[50] At the same time, Cyril reminds his readers that contemplation calls for imitation or emulation. We received the dignity of being stewards of God's creation; let us prove ourselves worthy of the title by striving to excel the abundant fields as we enrich ourselves with grace and virtue. If nature renews itself in spring, should we not renew ourselves at the coming of Easter?

> For it would truly be unthinkable that all growing plants and all kinds of trees regain their original appearance, while the people for whose sake the trees were created should lie destitute of the care of heavenly providence.[51]

The same thought runs throughout his twenty-ninth festal letter where he points out how absurd it would be if those who have been gifted with divine likeness suffered from spiritual sterility, while nature blossomed everywhere in spring.[52]

In his second festal letter Cyril calls spring the *epidemía* or sojourn of Jesus Christ on earth. The ancient Greeks imagined that spring brought divine salvation, while winter withdrew it; that spring was God's visit to the world, his *epidemía*, while winter was his *apodemía* or departure. Cyril adopts this to explain how the devil, like the winter storm that spreads gloom in our hearts, has been destroyed at the coming of Christ. The Savior who departed in winter has returned to make his home among us.[53] Or as Cyril puts it in his thirteenth festal letter, "Christ comes to us like the springtime on the mountain."[54] Springtime on top of the mountain is the first sign of nature's reawakening to life. In the same way, the apparition of

Christ in spring is the first sign and the assurance that our salvation is at hand. Every season is, of course, the sojourn of God among us; every season of the year is a season of grace. This is in fact the theological underpinning of the liturgical year. Yet spring possesses a particular realism and sacramental symbolism because of its association with Easter, the feast of feasts, and with the paschal mystery, the source of every grace.

Must Easter Be in Spring?

Spring is defined as the transitional period between winter and summer. In the northern hemisphere it comprises the months of March, April, and May. If reckoned astronomically, it extends from the equinox of March (the spring equinox) to the solstice of June (summer solstice). In the southern hemisphere the spring months fall in September, October, and December or from the equinox of September to the solstice of December. Thus while the church in the northern hemisphere is celebrating Easter in an atmosphere of new life and rebirth—provided, of course, winter does not usurp the spring months—the church in the southern hemisphere is witnessing the decline of nature's vitality. Surely autumn can be resplendent with its dazzling display of colors and pleasant in the mildness of its temperature. But who does not realize that in the cosmic cycle these are the rallying acts of a dying nature? In regions bordering on the tropical zone the church celebrates Easter either in the heat of summer or in the dampness of the wet season. Neither seems to provide the ideal condition for the celebration of the feast of our rebirth in Christ.[55]

And yet divine providence seems to have concentrated its attention on the northern hemisphere. Easter is a spring feast in every respect, from its origin and development to its ritual expressions. As a result there is a kind of symbiosis between the Christian feast and springtime. The qualities of one have been absorbed by the other. As we had the occasion to observe early on, spring has definitely enriched both the theology and liturgy of Easter. At the same time no season of the year has ever received as much lyrical praise in patristic literature as spring. Some writers were simply lavish in extolling it. The following text from St. Gregory of Nazianzus is a typical example of profuse praise: "Now is cosmic springtime; now is spiritual springtime, the springtime of souls, the springtime of the body; the visible spring, the invisible spring!"[56] We should not think that this and similar displays of unrestraint were under the influence of springtime itself. The Fathers must surely have delighted in the coming of spring, but the ultimate reason for jubilation was neither the end of winter nor the blossoming of nature but the celebration of Christ's resurrection.

Still we should not consider lightly the role of spring in the celebration of Easter.[57] Those who, rightly, put heavy stress on the spirituality of the feast might be tempted to dismiss the importance of the season, while those who view seasonal changes and manifestations with indifference might not see its relevance to Easter. It was not so with the Fathers of the church. For them Easter possessed a cosmic dimension. This means that they regarded spring as an integral part of the feast: it could not be celebrated at any other time of the year. We saw in the preceding chapter how the early church scrupulously observed the elements that made up the date of Easter. The first of these is the season of spring.

Must Easter be celebrated in spring? Theologically the answer rests on the concept of anniversary: spring marks the moment in time when Christ celebrated his own passover, that is, the mystery of his passion, death, and resurrection. It is therefore not a question of preference for one season over another, though spring has undeniably an advantage over the others because of its qualities and ability to portray in cosmic symbols the meaning of Easter. It is ultimately a question of authenticity or factual truth. Christian tradition is constant in affirming that Christ died and rose from the dead in spring; hence the church commemorates the event in spring. Since the event took place in the northern hemisphere, the reckoning of the date has, in consequence, been inseparably linked with the seasonal changes in that region of the world.

Celebrating Easter in spring also shows the continuity of this Christian feast with the Jewish feast of Passover and hence with the exodus. Although Easter is primarily the memorial of Christ's saving work, it does not forget the mighty deed of God when he led his people out of Egypt. God revealed and fulfilled his plan of salvation in stages, but there was continuity in his action. One event flowed into another or, in the manner of the biblical typology which we discussed early on in this work, one event foreshadowed and prepared for the next. This is the connection Christians perceive between the exodus of the Israelites and the paschal mystery of Christ. By celebrating

Easter at the season of the year when the exodus and Christ's sacrifice happened, the church affirms that these events are not disparate items in God's plan. Spring is the time element which links them together.

Thus spring reminds us of the *mirabilia Dei*, the wonders God accomplished in our world. In this sense we may predicate to spring a sacramental quality, that is, the ability to make us remember the plan of God and its fulfillment in Christ. Everytime spring comes around we witness, as it were, in the reality of a renewed creation the reality of our spiritual rebirth. Spring evokes and portrays through the stirring movement of an awakened creation the mystery of Christ's resurrecton from the dead. And because it has a sacramental quality, spring not only recalls the work of God; it also ushers in the new season of grace, or as St. Cyril of Alexandria puts it, "spring brings to us the resurrection of the Savior, by which he restored us to newness of life, after he had escaped the corruption of death."[58]

Spring evidently possesses the kind of symbols theology and liturgy can use to advantage. The church Fathers did avail of this, as we can see in their homilies, letters, and tracts on Easter. For who could miss the connection between the manifestations of springtime and the reality of our new life in Christ? But apart from the wealth of symbols it has in reserve, spring has the particular role of signaling the start of the Easter celebration, the anniversary anamnesis, the yearly memorial of the paschal mystery.

We draw from the foregoing considerations that spring has two roles, namely as an element of the Easter date and as an element of Easter symbolism. The feast is kept in spring in order to satisfy the requirement for an anniversary celebration: the feast should coincide with the date of Christ's passover. However, time is relative. When Christ died, it was spring in Palestine, but simultaneously autumn and summer in the southern and equatorial regions. Churches in these parts of the world comply with the principle of time concurrence when they celebrate Easter in autumn or summer. For them these are the seasons of Christ's death and resurrection. This is probably the basic consideration that should ultimately guide us when we deal with churches that have been "sentenced" by theology and liturgical tradition to celebrate Easter in autumn or summer.

Yet it would be liturgically and spiritually disastrous to ignore symbolism. What is Easter or, for that matter, any liturgical feast without symbols? It is evident that outside the northern hemisphere

Easter symbols need not, should not, be drawn from spring. We have labored too long under the impression that Easter is authentic when nature flourishes in youthful beauty and freshness. Had Christ died in autumn, the early Christian writers would have discovered in it such unsurpassable qualities as would win for it the title of *epidemía*, the sojourn of God among us. And the liturgy too would have adopted rites, formularies, and symbols that evoke creation's coming to maturity. We should not go on pretending that it is spring when it is actually fall or summer. We should not allow the paschal mystery to be indissolubly bound up with one season of the year. For indeed, every season of the year is the season of Christ's death and resurrection.

NOTES

1. M. Eliade, *The Sacred and the Profane* (New York 1955) 105; Eliade, *Cosmos and History* (New York 1959) 54.

2. I.H. Dalmais, "Theology of the Liturgical Celebration," in *The Church at Prayer*, vol. 1 (Collegeville 1987) 260.

3. English text in M. Eliade, *From Primitives to Zen* (London 1967) 98-108.

4. See Eliade, *Cosmos and History* 56-58; H. Gaster, *Thespis: Ritual, Myth and Drama in the Ancient Near East* (New York 1961) 61-64.

5. English text in M. Eliade, *Patterns in Comparative Religion* (London 1958) 404.

6. G. Yee, *Jewish Feasts and the Gospel of John* (Wilmington 1989) 28-29.

7. J. Van Goudoever, *Biblical Calendars* (Leiden 1961) 36-44; H.-J. Kraus, *Worship in Israel* (Oxford 1966) 61-70; A. Adam, *The Liturgical Year* (New York 1981) 12-13.

8. *Rosh ha-shana* I, 1, *The Mishnah* (London 1964) 188.

9. Philo of Alexandria, *The Special Laws II*, Loeb Classical Library, vol. 7 (Cambridge 1958) 150.

10. *Rosch ha-schana*, 10b-11a, *Der Babylonische Talmud* (Berlin 1930) 553.

11. *Berakot*, IX 59b, *Der Babylonische Talmud* 265.

12. J. Van Goudoever, *Biblical Calendars* 62-70. While the Book of Exodus supposes a calendar on which the first day of the first month falls on a Sunday, "the writer of the Book of Jubilees has projected a calendar-year which begins on a Wednesday."

13. Philo of Alexandria, *The Special Laws* II 399.

14. Ibid. 398.

15. M. Eliade, *Patterns in Comparative Religion* 400-401; H. Gaster, *Thespis* 61.

16. Q.J. Hilarian, *Expositum de Die Paschae et Mensis* (PL 13:1107-1108).

17. Philo of Alexandria, *The Special Laws* II 397.

18. Origen, *Commentary on Song of Songs* III (*PG* 13:182).

19. See Th. Michels, "Das Frühjahrssymbol in österlicher Liturgie," *Jahrbuch für Liturgiewissenschaft* 6 (1926) 7-11.

20. Eusebius of Caesarea, *The Feast of Easter* (PG 24:696). This treatise was written around the year 335 and was dedicated to Emperor Constantine. It discusses several issues regarding Easter, particularly the Nicene controversy and the eucharist as the Christian counterpart of the paschal meal.

21. Ibid.

22. Ibid.

23. For the concept of sacred time in antiquity, see G. Van der Leeuw, *Religion in Essence and Manifestation* (New York 1963); see also A. Rizzi, "Categorie culturali odierne nell'interpretazione del tempo," *L'Anno liturgico* (Casale Monferrato 1983) 11-22; M. Augé, "Il tempo nelle culture arcaiche," in *Anamnesis*, vol. 6 (Genoa 1988) 13-14.

24. Cyril of Jerusalem, *Catechetical Lectures* (PG 33:836); English translation in *The Works of St. Cyril of Jerusalem*, The Fathers of the Church, vol. 64 (Washington, D.C. 1970) 37-38.

25. Gregory of Nazianzus, *The New Sunday* (PG 36:617).

26. *Homélies pascales* I (ed. P. Nautin), *Sources chrétiennes*, vol. 27 (1950); see R. Cantalamessa, *L'Omelia "In S. Pascha" dello Pseudo-Ippolito di Roma* (Milan 1967).

27. Ibid. 145.

28. Gregory of Nazianzus, *On Holy Easter* II (PG 36:641).

29. Ambrose of Milan, *Exameron*, in *Opera Omnia di Sant'Ambrogio*, vol. 1 (Milan 1979).

30. Ibid. I, 4:12-14, pp. 34-38.

31. Ibid., 4:14, p. 38; cf. Augustine, *De Cain et Abel*, Corpus Scriptorum Ecclesiasticorum Latinorum, vol. 33 (1897) 366; Zeno of Verona, *Tractatus XLV de Die Dominico Paschatis* (PL 11:501); Maximus of Turin, *Sermo LVI de Pentecosten*, Corpus Christianorum Latinorum, vol. 23 (1962) 224.

32. Pseudo-Ambrose, *Sermo de Dominica Resurrectione* (PL 17:695); cf. Augustine of Hippo, *Enarrationes i Psalmis*, Corpus Christianorum Latinorum, vol. 40 (1956) 1791: "Per passionem enim transiit Dominus a morte ad vitam; et fecit nobis viam credentibus in resurrectionem eius, ut transeamus et nos de morte ad vitam." See the classic article of C. Mohrmann, "Pascha, Passio, Transitus," *Ephemerides Liturgicae* 66 (1952) 37-52.

33. Ibid., 4:13, p. 36. The theme of cosmogony in spring is found in several patristic writings, e.g., Nicetas of Remesiana, *De Ratione Paschae* (Cambridge 1905) 98: "Resurrexit enim Christus in aequinnoctio veris, luna plena, die dominica: quae in mundi convenire principium Genesis relatione cognoscimus." See also *Acta Synodi Caesariensis*, in *Studi e Testi* 59 (1933) 22-23; Pseudo-Ambrose, *Sermo XXXV de Mysterio Paschae* II (PL 17:695).

34. Gaudentius of Brescia, *Tractatus Paschales, Tractatus I in Exodum*, Corpus Scriptorum Ecclesiasticorum Latinorum, vol. 68 (1936) 18.

35. Ibid. 19. Since Christ is supposed to have risen in the month of March, Gaudentius justifies the celebration of Easter in April, the second month, on grounds that Law allowed a second Passover.

36. Nicetas of Remesiana, *De Ratione Paschae* 94.

37. Leo the Great, *De Passione Domini Sermo IX*, Sources chrétiennes, vol. 74bis (1976) 124; see also Eusebius of Caesarea, *The Feast of Easter* (PG 24:698).

38. *Acta Synodi Caesariensis* 22.

39. For the latest study on Apponius, see L. Crociani, *Apponii in Canticum Canticorum Explanationes Libri VI. Tradizione del testo, fonti, liturgia, teologia* (Rome 1991).

40. Apponius, *In Canticum Canticorum Expositio*, Corpus Christianorum Latinorum, vol. 19 (1986) 100.

41. *Rosch ha-schana, Der Babylonische Talmud* 553; see J. Van Goudoever, *Biblical Calendars* 130-131.

42. Melito of Sardis: *Homily on Easter*, Sources chrétiennes, vol. 123 (1966) 99-111.

43. See N. Füglister, "The Biblical Roots of the Easter Celebration," in *Celebrating the Easter Vigil* (New York 1983) 3-35; A. Saldarini, *Jesus and Passover* (New York 1984) 101-105.

44. Apponius, *In Canticum Canticorum Explanationes*.

45. *Book of Jubilees*, 19:5; 17:5; 18:1-17, 27:19.

46. Cyril of Alexandria, *Festal Letters* (PG 77). Festal or Easter letters were pastoral letters sent by Alexandrian bishops to the churches in Egypt to announce the date of Easter Sunday and the Lenten fasts. See H. Rahner, "Österliche Frühlingslyrik bei Kyrillos von Alexandreia," in *Paschatis Sollemnia* (Freiburg 1959) 68-75.

47. Cyril of Alexandria, *Festal Letter IX* (PG 77:581).

48. *Festal Letter XIV* (PG 77:709).

49. *Festal Letter XVI* (PG 77:752).

50. Ibid.

51. *Festal Letter IX* (PG 77:581).

52. *Festal Letter XXIX* (PG 77:960); cf. Basil of Seleucia, *On Holy Easter*, Sources chrétiennes, vol. 187 (1972) 206-214.

53. *Festal Letter II* (PG 77:432).

54. *Festal Letter XIII* (PG 77:695).

55. A similar difficulty, though liturgically much less problematic, occurs in the celebration of Christmas. Though it is traditionally associated with the winter solstice, it is celebrated in the southern hemisphere in December when it is summer.

56. Gregory of Nazianzus, *On the New Sunday* (PG 36:617).

57. See H. Rahner, "Österlicher Frühling," *Wort und Wahrheit* 4 (1949) 241-248.

58. Cyril of Alexandria, *Festal Letters IX* (PG 77:581).

Chapter Three
Easter and the Spring Equinox

Spring Equinox and the Easter Date

Equinox comes from two Latin words, *aequa* (equal) and *nox* (night). It is the point on the celestial sphere where the celestial equator intersects the ecliptic. Twice a year the sun, which moves in the ecliptic, crosses the celestial equator, once toward the north about 21 March when it enters the zodiac of Aries (vernal or spring equinox), and once toward the south about 23 September (autumnal equinox). At either of these points of intersection the sun is directly over the earth's equator, and day and night are everywhere of equal length. To determine the correct date of Easter in any given year, the first step is to know when the spring equinox will occur. In the past this has often not been an easy task. Easter calendars and tables based on different lunar and solar cycles were invented in view of lessening or resolving the difficulty of setting the Easter date. Often they muddled even more an already confused issue. For many centuries the reckoning of the date of Easter was an object of considerable debate in the church.[1]

A highly respected Easter table, from which the church of Alexandria never departed, was composed by Anatolius of Laodicea toward the year 270 A.D. on the basis of the lunar calendar discovered by Metonius in 432 B.C. This calendar, which in antiquity had the distinction of being called "the golden number," consisted of a cycle of nineteen years comprising 235 lunations. The cycle of nineteen years was subsequently developed into a cycle of ninety-five years (19 x 5) and became the basis of the Easter table in the west from 437 to 1581. Another widely known table was the one based on a cycle of twenty-eight years (7 x 4), the *circulus solis*, which was in reality a cycle of weeks. Seven stands for the number of years it would take the first day of the year to fall again on the same day of the week, while four represents the leap year. The *laterculus augustalis* consisting of eighty-four years (28 x 3) was formed from this cycle and was used in Rome from the fourth to the fifth century. Other notable Easter tables were the Hippolytan table of 16 years and its revised form of 112 years (16 x 7), the table of eight years used in both the east and the west at the beginning of the third century, the fifth-century "perfect" table of Victor of Aquitaine, which was a lunisolar calendar of 532 years that spread quickly in the west as far as remote Ireland, and the famous Easter table of Dionysius Exiguus.

Each of these Easter calendars or tables employed a particular astronomical apparatus, at times inaccurate, though often corroborated with biblical authority. Obviously there were different reasons for accepting or rejecting a given calendar. Sometimes they had nothing to do with the astronomical precision of the calendar in question. The seventh-century *Chronicon Paschale*, for instance, strongly defends the Alexandrian cycle of nineteen years, because it was sanctioned by the Council of Nicea. It severely criticizes the cycle of ninety-five years which, it claims, is the reason why pagans and Jews ridicule Christian Easter. It scorns the cycle of 532 for ignoring the "faith of the church" and affirms that the cycle of nineteen years is the only correct one. It notes that when correlated with the cycle of twenty-eight years, the cycle of nineteen years has the advantage of always beginning on 21 March.[2]

The Julian reform of 45 B.C. fixed the spring equinox on 25 March. By 325 A.D., at the Council of Nicea, the Alexandrians were observing it on 21 March. In the sixteenth century the spring equinox had slipped down to 11 March. To adjust it to the true solar course the Gregorian reform of 1582 suppressed ten days from the calendar. Although the Council of Nicea had already adopted 21 March, the Roman Church, which was less familiar than the Alexandrian with the intricate science of astronomy, continued to observe 25 March subserviently for several years after the council.[3] In 346 it refused to celebrate Easter Sunday before 25 March on grounds that the spring equinox had not yet passed.

But even after Rome had finally accepted 21 March as the equinox and shifted the lower limit of the Easter date from 26 March to 22 March, its Easter tables up to the time of St. Isidore of Seville, who died in 636, consistently exhibited 25 March as the spring equinox. The confusion grew worse when Rome tried to tally its table with that of Alexandria. Rome understood 22 March as the lower limit for Easter Sunday, and hence 21 April as the upper limit beyond which it was not lawful to celebrate Easter. However, for the Alexandrian Church 22 March was the lower limit not for Easter Sunday but for 14 Nisan or the spring full moon. Since the Easter canon did not permit the celebration of the feast until after the full moon, the Alexandrian table had to give a margin of four additional days to the upper limit. In other words, the Alexandrian *mensis novorum* or "first month" had thirty-five days running from 22 March through 25 April. Rome considered this an excessively protracted month.

Between Rome and Alexandria the limits of the "first month" within which Easter could be lawfully celebrated had a difference of five days. Basically the difference stemmed from the inability of Rome to figure out exactly what the Alexandrians meant by lunar year and "first month." Gaudentius of Brescia, for example, thought that "first month" meant March, and hence had difficulty explaining why Easter was sometimes celebrated in April.[4] Nevertheless, the Alexandrian upper limit did not always go uncontested in other Oriental Churches, despite assurances that it came from the apostles or at least from the Council of Nicea.[5] Even for these Churches thirty-five days seemed too long for one month. In 387 Alexandria marked 25 April in its calendar as Easter Sunday. In Anatolia, where the Alexandrian calendar was being followed, there were protests against this considerable delay, which the famous *Easter Homily* of 387 sought to justify. The homilist based his argument on the canon of Nicea forbidding the celebration of Easter Sunday before the passing of the spring equinox and the full moon. Since in the year 387 the equinox fell on Sunday, 21 March, and the full moon on Sunday, 18 April, there was no option but to move the date of Easter Sunday to 25 April.[6]

The preceding year the bishops of the province of Aemilia in North Italy, who had come to learn about the Alexandrian Easter date, conferred with St. Ambrose of Milan. Ambrose endorsed 25 April. We gather from the letter he sent to the bishops that Milan and the province of Aemilia followed the Roman *mensis novorum* consisting of thirty-one days. The problem arose when they collated this with the Alexandrian calendar. Ambrose explained to the bishops that "the *mensis novorum* is not reckoned according to common usage, but according to the tradition of experts. It extends from the equinox on the XII Kalends of April to the XI Kalends of May. It is within these thirty-one days that the feast of Easter is normally (*saepe*) celebrated."[7] It could happen, as it would the following year, that Easter Sunday fell outside the thirty-one days fixed by the Roman table. Ambrose assured the bishops that there was no cause for anxiety, because 25 April, though outside the Roman limit, was still within the Alexandrian *mensis novorum*. We can detect in the letter a certain attitude of ambivalence toward Roman tradition as well as the freedom to celebrate either with the Romans or with the Alexandrians. Ambrose informed the bishops that in 387 "we shall keep Easter Sunday in the first month according to the Egyptians, that is, on the VII Kalends of May which is the thirtieth day of the month of Pharmuthi."[8]

Easter Sunday in Rome in 387 cannot be dated with precision. The table for that year offered a choice between two dates, 21 March or 18 April. In view of Rome's rigid principle not to celebrate until after the passing of the spring equinox, it is probable that the feast that year was held on 18 April. But then it must have coincided with 14 Nisan, that is, with the Jewish Passover, an eventuality Rome must have accepted most grudgingly.[9] In due course the Roman Church adopted the Alexandrian upper limit as well, so that now Easter Sunday can actually fall as early as 22 March and as late as 25 April. The last time Easter Sunday fell on 22 March was in 1761 and again in 1818. It will not do so in the twentieth and twenty-first centuries. The last time it fell on 25 April was in 1943 and will again in 2038.

We made reference to an Easter canon which requires that Easter should not be celebrated before spring equinox shall have passed. Some church Fathers claimed that the Council of Nicea sanctioned this canon, but the conciliar document on the matter, if there had been any, is irretrievably lost. What we know is that, besides the condemnation of Arius, the Easter date was tackled by the council in order to check the "scandal of divergent practices."[10] Epiphanius of Salamis reports that "already in ancient times there existed in the church various controversies and disagreements regarding this feast, and every year they caused laughter and ridicule."[11]

During the first three centuries there had been several groups of Christians in Asia Minor who held on tenaciously to the Jewish paschal calendar. They celebrated Easter on 14 Nisan, the day of the full moon, regardless of whether or not it fell on Sunday or after the spring equinox.[12] They were indiscriminately called Quartodecimans (from 14 Nisan), giving the impression that they formed one community. In reality they were communities scattered in different parts of Asia Minor and as far as Gaul. Even among those who kept Easter on Sunday there was, as we have seen early on, no unity in the issue of equinox, in as much as some fixed it on 21 March, while others on 25 March. It seems that the objective of the Council of Nicea was not to impose a uniform system of reckoning the passing of the equinox, but to eliminate the Quartodeciman observance. The personal letter sent by Emperor Constantine to all the bishops regarding the decision of the council gives a strong indication of a feeling of uneasiness with the lingering presence of Judaism in the church. "It was agreed upon by all," Constantine informs the bishops, "that it would truly be an unworthy thing for us to follow the practice of the Jews in the celebration of this holy feast. Let us therefore have nothing in common with the cursed race of the Jews."[13]

The overriding concern to rid the church of Jewish paschal practices needed to be complemented. The church should show unity in the way it celebrates the feast of Easter. As normally happens in general conventions where particulars are overlooked, in the Council of Nicea the mechanics for determining the Easter date were not discussed. No Easter table was sanctioned by the council, and its only tangible achievement was the consensus reached by the bishops, that henceforth Easter shall be kept after the spring equinox. The letter of Constantine informs us that "after mature deliberation on the problem concerning the date of Easter it was decreed by common consent that this feast ought to be celebrated everywhere on the same day (*epi mias heméras*)."[14]

A council document edited by John the Scholastic of Constantinople in the sixth century reports that Nicea did not touch the question of the equinox at any detailed length, but "left aside all research and debate." The council was not interested in the intricate science of lunar cycles and Easter tables. Its chief aim was to put pressure on the Quartodecimans to abandon the Jewish calendar, "and to do as the Romans and Alexandrians and all the rest do," that is, to celebrate Easter after the vernal equinox.[15] We observe in passing that the question of imposing Sunday as the day of Easter does not appear to have been the centerpiece of the conciliar discussion. It would seem that for what the council aimed it was enough that Christians did not follow the Jewish computation of the spring equinox.

The letter of the council to the churches in Alexandria furnishes us with more information:

> We send you the joyful news of the unanimous agreement on the celebration of the feast of Easter. Thanks to your prayers, the issue is now rightly settled, so that all the brethren in Asia who formerly imitated the Jews shall henceforth celebrate the feast in perfect accord with the Romans and with you and with us all who from the beginning have kept the same practice with you.[16]

History offers evidence that "to celebrate the feast in perfect accord" did not mean "everywhere on the same day," as Constantine's letter ordained. There had been instances when Rome did not agree with Alexandria. In 349 the Alexandrian table set Easter Sunday on 23 April. Rome, which still observed the upper limit on 21 April, objected, and through the diplomacy of St. Athanasius the Church of Alexandria agreed to celebrate Easter with Rome on 26 March. The same happened in 444, but this time Rome could not persuade Alexandria.

The church has sometimes been censured for what has been called its "anti-Judaic motivation" or "strong anti-Judaic feelings."[17] In the case of the Easter date the church's "repudiation of the Jewish reckoning of Passover" had a more substantial reason than mere sentiments of antipathy. The letter of Constantine sheds light on this. It points out that the Jews "err seriously in intercalation [of additional month] and thus celebrate two Passovers in one year."[18] The curious occurrence of two Passovers or, for the Quartodecimans, two Easter celebrations in the course of one liturgical year was blamed on erroneous system of intercalation. This sometimes resulted in a calendar that marked 14 Nisan even before the spring equinox. Anatolius of Laodicea wrote that the original practice of the Jews since time immemorial was the celebration of Passover after the equinox.[19] And Peter of Alexandria informed the Quartodeciman Terentius that "the ancients appear to have kept the feast after the spring equinox. This you can find out, if you read ancient books, especially those written by learned Hebrews."[20] Two Easter celebrations in a single year must have been a cause of distress and embarrassment for the church. This is the background of the Council of

Nicea's declaration that "henceforth we shall not tolerate a second Easter to be celebrated in one year."[21]

In a calendar in which the year is reckoned from January to December, it is not possible to repeat Easter twice in a year, even if it is kept before spring equinox. But in a calendar that runs from one spring equinox to another the phenomenon of a double Easter can quite easily happen every other year or so, if it is held regardless of the equinox. To illustrate, let us assume that in a given year the full moon rises after the spring equinox. This will correctly be considered the Easter full moon and hence the feast will be held at the beginning of that year. Supposing that before the end of the year the full moon rises just before the next spring equinox, and it is mistakenly reckoned as the Easter full moon, Easter will be celebrated a second time within the span of one year. And the odd thing about this system is that in the year that follows, which is ordinarily intercalated so that the full moon rises only after the spring equinox, there will be no Easter at all.

This in so many words is what Epiphanius of Salamis, that intransigent defender of orthodoxy, tried to explain in a treatise against the group of Audianians who, besides harboring some intolerable heresies, were also Quartodecimans. "If we celebrate with them," he warns, "we shall have two Easters in the same year, one before and another after the equinox. And the year after we will not celebrate even one Easter."[22] In an earlier treatise against another group of heretics Epiphanius explains that the church

> observes not only the fourteenth day of the moon but also the course of the sun, lest we celebrate two Easters in the course of the same year and none in the next. We therefore take into account only the full moon which rises after the equinox.[23]

We note the same concern in the *Apostolic Constitutions* written toward the end of the fourth century. Chapter 17 of its fifth book contains the norms for implementing in the Syrian Church the decrees of the Council of Nicea. Its canon on the Easter date reads:

> You shall keep accurately and diligently the day of Easter after the equinox, otherwise you will celebrate twice in the year the memory of one passion. Once a year you shall celebrate the memory of him who died only once.[24]

The argument is feebly premised on the pauline doctrine of *ephapax*, but it is solidly built on the principle of anamnesis. Although every Sunday is the anamnesis of the resurrection, the church linked the memory of Christ's paschal mystery more closely with the yearly than with the weekly cycle, in much the same way as we would spontaneously link an event, like a birthday, wedding, or death, with the year rather than with the week. Yet it would surely be strange, if we kept an anniversary twice during the year. This in effect was what the Quartodecimans introduced into the church. And so the *Apostolic Constitutions* exhorted that "you shall no longer observe the feast of Easter with the Jews; we should no longer keep *koinonia* with them."[25] Infringement of this canon carried a heavy penalty: "If any bishop, presbyter, or deacon celebrates the holy day of Easter before the spring equinox, at the same time with the Jews, let him be deposed."[26]

The Symbolism of Spring Equinox

The canon regarding the celebration of Easter after the spring equinox was an effective measure against the anomaly of two Easters in the course of one liturgical year. But the interest of early Christian writers was not confined to this disciplinary aspect of the question. The spring equinox, with its mystique of equal length of day and night, enticed them to discover the deeper meaning of this cosmic phenomenon.

The author of the anonymous *Easter Homily* of 387 expounds with the consummate skill of a Greek theorist the relation between the spring equinox and cosmogony. He invites his listeners to "consider the creation of God and find out for yourselves that the equinox came first at the beginning of time," that is, when God divided the first day and night into equal parts.[27] Harmony and balance among the elements were the distinguishing marks of nature's primordial passage from chaos to cosmos. To prove that God created time in the state of equilibrium the homilist invokes the authority of Philo of Alexandria, the "learned Hebrew." But that state did not last. As soon as God put day and night into motion, inequality set in: the length of day no longer equaled the length of night. Where do we find the original equilibrium between day and night? We must go back in time to the exact moment of cosmogony, before any element went into motion. For at the start of every motion there is a state of equilibrium, or in the words of the homilist, "if inequality comes with motion, equilibrium characterizes creation."[28]

The spring equinox, our homilist affirms, is the faithful image of the moment of cosmogony, the state of cosmic equilibrium at the start of creation. In support of this belief he refers his listeners to the account of Genesis 1:3 which says that God separated light from darkness. We note in passing that this scriptural passage was the *locus classicus* employed by early Christian writers and authors of Easter tables to prove respectively the validity of their doctrine and computation. Ironically Exodus 12 was not of much help for determining the Easter date.

The symbolism of spring equinox as *caput temporis* or the beginning of time was popular among Latin writers. It is amazing how they, more than their Greek peers, valued Genesis 1. One might suggest that this was due in part to their limited familiarity with the science of astronomy. What caught their attention was the equal division between light and darkness, a clear proof for them that God created the world at the spring equinox.

Pioneering in this art was a Pseudo-Cyprian who lived in Africa before the second half of the third century. His work, which revises the Easter table of Hippolytus, has come down to us under the title *De Pascha Computus*. It sets haphazardly the Easter limits between 19 March and 20 April and fixes the equinox on 25 March, thus consenting to the celebration of Easter before the spring equinox. Apparently the Church of Rome followed this table until the year 312, when it adopted the cycle of eighty-four years.[29] But apart from this negative observation, Pseudo-Cyprian has the distinction of being the first to make use of the creation narrative of Genesis 1 to give authoritative sanction to his work. Probably the first of its kind in the Latin world, his method influenced succeeding generations until the time of Bede the Venerable. According to Pseudo-Cyprian, if we wish to know when Nisan or the Easter *mensis novorum* begins and ends, "we must first examine Genesis, which narrates that God himself separated the first day from the first night."

Within the range of Pseudo-Cyprian's influence was a certain Quintus Hilarian who lived toward the end of the fourth century. In his treatise called *Expositum de Die Paschae et Mensis* he writes: "Reason compels us to review the origin of the world, in order to determine the first month set aside by the Law for the celebration of

Easter."[30] For in the Egyptian and Roman calendars the first month of the year began respectively on the IV Kalends of September and the Kalends of January, while the Easter *mensis novorum* began in the month of Nisan. To reckon the first month prescribed by Exodus 12 for the feast of Passover, we are told by Hilarian to examine the creation account of Genesis 1. The spurious *Acta Synodi Caesariensis* advocated the same procedure: "We must first inquire when the world was created, and when this shall have been diligently studied, then we can establish correctly the canon on Easter date."[31]

Spring equinox is related not only to cosmogony but also to the paschal mystery of Christ. The patristic literature dealing with this latter subject is quite complex, due in part to a double tradition regarding the VIII Kalends of April or 25 March which was the Julian equinox. One tradition assigned to this day the passion and death of Christ, while the other took the resolute stand that it was the day when he rose from the dead.

With great precision Nicetas of Remesiana affirms that "Christ rose from the dead at the spring equinox, when it was full moon, on Sunday. From the narration of Genesis we learn that this time coincided with the beginning of the world."[32] Nicetas adds that "Christ rose indeed on the VIII Kalends of April," or 25 March which he regards as the day of the equinox. We note in passing that, though the lower limit of the Easter table in the west had already, by this time, that is, the beginning of the fifth century, been fixed to 22 March, several Easter tables continued to mark 25 March as the equinox. For Nicetas 25 March was, however, not the first day of creation. According to him, it is the XI Kalends of April or 22 March: "For before the sun was created to head the day, three days had passed. In fact the Book of Genesis says that the lights of the sun and the moon were created on the fourth day." It is obvious that Nicetas mistakenly took the equinox to mean, not the first day of creation, but the fourth day when the sun and the moon were created. St. Cyril of Jerusalem shares this understanding of the equinox provided by biblical astronomy.[33]

If Christ rose from the dead on 25 March, the chronology of the paschal events would be as follows: he ate the supper with his disciples on 22 March, suffered and died on 23 March, and lay in the tomb on 24 March. Nicetas realized that these three days fell before the equinox and hence ran the risk of technically not being considered part of the Easter celebration. In his time the Easter triduum already included Holy Thursday. To solve the problem Nicetas broadened the concept of equinox to include the three days preceding the creation of the sun and the moon:

> He rose indeed on the VIII Kalends of April, although he ate the supper with his disciples on the XI Kalends of April. Hence, these three days share in his passion and resurrection, and the spring equinox is understood to include the three days before the sun and the moon went on their course.[34]

It is possible that Nicetas had another and an ulterior motive for extending the equinox to the three preceding days. It was his way of justifying those instances in the west when Easter Sunday fell, according to the Alexandrian computation but contrary to the post-equinoctial canon, before the Julian equinox of 25 March.

The author of the *Acta Synodi Caesariensis* faced the same problem. He also fixed the spring equinox on 25 March, the first day of creation and the first day of the week. For him there was no question that Christ rose from the dead on 25 March. His difficulty was how to explain the fact that the three extra days from 22 March to 24 March, which preceded, according to his biblical astronomy, the days of cosmogony, had been incorporated into the Easter table. Like Nicetas of Remesiana, he cleverly solved the problem by invoking the tradition that Christ suffered, died, and was buried in the course of those three days. He writes:

> Bishop Theophilus said, Is it not impious to exclude from the Easter month the three days of the Lord's passion, which is such a great mystery? For our Lord began his suffering on the XI Kalends of April, on the fifth day which we call the Lord's Supper.

The bishops of the synod all agreed that there was no reason why so great a mystery should be left out of the Easter celebration. "Hence, it was decided in that synod that they should keep Easter after the XI Kalends of April and before the XI Kalends of May."[35]

The other tradition fixes the passion and death of Christ on 25 March. One early document that mentions this is the apocryphal *Acts of Pilate*.[36] We may surmise that 25 March was chosen as the day of Christ's death because it was the day of the equinox in the Julian calendar. Probably for the same reason the other tradition fixed the date of the resurrection also on this day. The Quartodecimans, whose Easter theology stressed the passion and death of Christ, based their calendar on the *Acts of Pilate*, while those, whose Easter celebration focused on the resurrection, did much to propagate the other tradition. We learn from Ephiphanius of Salamis that on the authority of the *Acts of Pilate* some communities of Quartodecimans always kept Easter on 25 March, regardless of the day of the week and of 14 Nisan, or else they simply declared every 25 March to be 14 Nisan. "They are proud of the fact that they received this practice from the *Acts of Pilate* which mentions that the Savior suffered on the VIII Kalends of April."[37]

But as T. Talley has pointed out, "those texts that assign the resurrection, rather than the passion, to March 25 clearly represent a secondary stratum, an adjustment to the shifting content of Pascha." He adds that "the older and more constant current in the tradition assigns the passion to that date and sees it as a coincidence of the Julian date with 14 Nisan, the Preparation of the Passover, following the Johannine passion chronology."[38] This is confirmed by a statement of Hilarian who lived toward the end of the fourth century: "Christ the Lord suffered on the fourteenth day of the month [of Nisan], on the VIII Kalends of April, on the sixth day."[39]

The author of the *Easter Homily* of 387, though by no means a Quartodeciman sympathizer, accepted the tradition of 25 March. After sharply denouncing the Jews and the Quartodecimans for their pre-equinoctial practice, he produced the *Acts of Pilate* in support of the post-equinoctial canon. He reminded his listeners that Easter must be celebrated after the equinox, because Christ died after the equinox.

> In fact the date of the Savior's suffering is not unknown, as this date is mentioned in the *Acts of Pilate*. It is written there that our Savior suffered on the VIII Kalends of April. This day comes after the equinox, and is accepted as such by experts.[40]

Since the Alexandrian equinox was on 21 March and the passion of Christ was on 25 March, the homilist of 387 had no difficulty whatever in asserting the validity of the Nicene canon.

A fascinating topic which our homilist developed is the *anakephala2osis* or recapitulation of the entire creation in the paschal mystery of Christ. According to him, "in his plan to refashion the human race the Son of God made it his particular concern to observe the primordial time when the first human beings were created and fell into sin."[41] The primordial time he was referring to was the first week of creation, particularly the first, fourth, and sixth day. The spring equinox, full moon, and Friday needed to converge in the same week, in order to recapture the image of the primordial week described by Genesis. As long as this did not obtain, Christ escaped from the hand of his enemies. He escaped, not out of fear of death, but out of a desire to make the week of his passover coincide with the week of cosmogony.

> But when the Son of God had finally gathered these elements together, when he had finished planning the week of his passion according to the original week of creation, and when the equinox, full moon, and Friday had finally come together, then he de-livered himself up to suffering.[42]

What impelled Christ to do this? The homilist explains that the time created by God in the beginning was pure, but the sin of the first parents defiled it. He pictures time as a spring that flows from a source. Any defilement in the source is carried over to the streams. In order to cleanse time Christ needed to take hold of its initial point whence his purifying action could flow into the succeeding ages. By dying on the day when the equinox, full moon, and Friday converged in perfect imitation of the cosmogonic week, he recapitulated time and the cosmos, and he gathered them under one head, that is, himself. For the homilist the aim of *anakephalaíosis* or recapitulation is to bring about the unity of earth with heaven and to assemble together all created beings under the renewing power of his death. That is why

> in his passion Christ observed the equinox, for the primordial time had to be recaptured; and he also observed Friday, for the first parents were formed on that day, and it was necessary that they be reformed on the day on which they were created and fell into sin.[43]

An anonymous and little known work called *De Paschate Iudaeorum*, which exists in Latin, though probably it was originally written in Greek, develops an impressive Easter typology of the spring equi-nox.[44] The author contrasts the first equinox with the new equinox, the first creation with the second creation, and the Jewish Passover with Christ's death. Concerning the typological meaning of the equinox, he writes: "The creation of the world at the first equinox was a figure which received fulfillment in the last equinox and in the passover of Christ." He regards the first equinox as a prophetic type presaging the renewal and redemption of the world, which was realized by Christ through his passion and death. This is the new equinox. By *aequinoctium novissimum* the author does not refer to something which has yet to come, but to something which has already come, to something which is new and also final. In the light of this reflection, we may say that we now experience the final equinox, that is, we live in the era of fulfillment. By his death Christ has brought the world to its final stage. The yearly advent of the spring equinox is a reminder of this great truth.

The Nicene canon of celebrating Easter after the passing of the spring equinox contributed also to the development of another Easter theme, namely the feast of light. Due in large measure to the Quartodeciman controversy, the church forbade the celebration of Easter on the day itself of the equinox. The symbolism behind this new legislation did not escape the attention of several early Christian writers. In fact in terms of symbols they found it more meaningful to celebrate the feast after the spring equinox. For during equinox there is an uneasy tension between light and darkness. They are still of equal length and force; neither has as yet won or lost. Until the tension is resolved in favor of light, the feast of light cannot be held meaningfully. In view of this new symbolism some writers did not glorify the spring equinox as the picture of harmony and tranquility.

The anonymous author of *Canon Paschalis* goes so far as to underrate the symbolic value of the spring equinox for the feast of Easter. He writes: "During the equinox the Easter festivity should not be held, because as long as the sun and the moon are in equinoctial position, the power of darkness is not yet overcome."[45] Another disadvantage he sees in celebrating at the spring equinox is that at this time the full moon does not shine the whole night, since it rises only when darkness has covered the earth. If Easter is the feast of light, it should be celebrated only in total light.

Another early Christian writer who treated the theme of light drawn from the equinox was Gregory of Nyssa. In his fourth letter dealing with Easter he develops the symbolism of the post-equinoctial celebration, although his point of reference is the equal length of day and night. In the elevated language typical of his writings he extols the power of Christ's glorious light to influence our lives:

The feast of the resurrection, which comes at a time when nights and days are of equal length, makes us understand that goodness does not need any longer to struggle with equal arms against an hostile army. Luminous life has triumphed, after having scattered the darkness of idolatry in the abundance of its light.[46]

Spring equinox played a major role in the development of the patristic theology of Easter. This theology is built on the premise that Christ died and rose again during the week that coincided with the first week of cosmogony. Putting stock in the "historical" value of the Genesis account, a good number of the early Christian writers attached special significance to the first, the fourth, and the sixth day of creation. The first day was marked by the spring equinox, the fourth day by the full moon, and the sixth day by the creation of the first man and woman. Tradition also has it that the first parents sinned and died on Friday.

For the Jewish people the advent of the spring equinox and the rising of the full moon indicated the season for the celebration of the Passover. For Christ they signaled the moment to pass from this world to the Father. Finally, for the early church they were the indicants of another season of grace. Christ's death on the sixth day and his resurrection on the first heightened even more the church's belief that by his paschal mystery Christ recasted the drama of creation. As a number of early Christian authors often pointed out, it was not mere coincidence that Christ died and rose again in the week corresponding to the week of creation: everything had been planned by God. The church's observance of the equinox is a re-sounding proclamation that the God of Genesis is the God of Exodus, that the Creator of the world is its Savior. The paschal mystery of Christ said it all.

NOTES

1. See Chauve-Bertrand, *La Question de Pâque et du calendrier* (Paris 1936) 67-95; C. Jones, *Bedae Opera de Temporibus* (Cambridge 1943) 6-55; N. Dennis-Boulet, *Le Calendrier chrétien* (Paris 1959) 20-25.

2. *Chronicon Paschale* (PG 92:85-96); see article of D. Stiernon, "Chronicon Paschale," *Dizionario patristico e di antichità christiane*, vol. 1 (Casale Monferrato 1983) 663-664.

3. The *Canon Paschalis* attributed to Anatolius of Laodicea (c. 270 A.D.) puts the beginning of the "first month" on 26 Phamenoth for the Alexandrians, 22 Dystri for the Macedonians, and mistakenly on the XI Kalends of April (22 March) for the Romans; see Eusebius of Caesarea, *History of the Church* VII, 32, Sources chrétiennes, vol. 41 (1955) 225.

4. Gaudentius of Brescia, *Tractatus Paschales. Tractatus I in Exodum*, Corpus Scriptorum Ecclesiasticorum Latinorum, vol. 68 (1936) 20.

5. The African *Praefatio Cyrilli* (c. 450 A.D.) claims that the Apostles observed Easter on a Sunday between 21 March and 25 April; see *Chronicon Paschale* (PG 92:548); C. Jones, *Bedae Opera de Temporibus* 40.

6. *Homélies Pascales III* (ed. F. Floeri - P. Nautin), Sources chrétiennes, vol. 48 (1957) 166.

7. Ambrose of Milan, *Epistola XXIII* (PL 16:1075).

8. Ibid.

9. See "Pâques," *Dictionnaire d'archéologie chrétienne et de liturgie*, vol. 13, 2 (1938) 1554.

10. Ibid. 1541; see L. Duchesne, "La question de la pâque au Concile de Nicée," *Revue des questions historiques* 28 (1880) 26-42; A. Adam, *The Liturgical Year* (New York 1981) 59; T. Talley, *The Origins of the Liturgical Year* (New York 1986) 216-218.

11. Epiphanius of Salamis, *Panarion*. Heresy 70. *Die Griechischen christlichen Schriftsteller der ersten drei Jahrhunderte*, vol. 37 (1933) 242.

12. F. Brightam, "The Quartodeciman Question," *Journal of Theological Studies* 15 (1924) 254-270; B. Lohse, *Das Passafest der Quartadecimaner* (Gütersloh 1953); B. Botte, "La question pascale: pâque du vendredi ou pâque du dimanche?," *La Maison-Dieu* 41 (1955) 84-95; M. Richard, "La question pascale au IIe siècle," *L'Orient Syrien* 6 (1961) 177-212; W. Huber, *Passa und Ostern. Untersuchungen zur Osterfeier der alten Kirche* (Berlin 1969); S. Bacchiocchi, *From Sabbath to Sunday* (Rome 1977) 198-207; T. Talley, *The Origins of the Liturgical Year* 5-13.

13. The text of the letter is in Eusebius of Caesarea: *Life of Constantine*, Die Griechischen christlichen Schriftsteller, vol. 9 (1902) 85-86. For the authenticity of the letter, see N. Baynes, "Constantine and the Christian Church," *Proceedings of the British Academy*, vol. 15 (1929) 89; see also S. Bacchiocchi, *From Sabbath to Sunday* 198-207.

14. Eusebius of Caesarea, *Life of Constantine* 85; cf. *Chronicon Paschale* (PG 92:84).

15. The text is in "Pâques," *Dictionnaire d'archéologie chrétienne et de liturgie*, vol. 13, 2, p. 1549.

16. The text is in *Mansi*, vol. 2 (a. 305-46) 911.

17. S. Bacchiocchi, *From Sabbath to Sunday* 206.

18. Eusebius of Caesarea, *Life of Constantine* 85.

19. Eusebius of Caesarea, *History of the Church* VII, p. 226.

20. *Fragments on Easter Celebration* (PG 18:517).

21. Eusebius of Caesarea, *Life of Constantine* 85.

22. Epiphanius of Salamis, *Panarion*. Heresy 70, pp. 244-245.

23. Ibid., Heresy 50, p. 248.

24. *Apostolic Constitutions* V, 17. Text in *Didascalia et Constitutiones Apostolorum*, ed. F.X. Funk (Paderborn 1905) 287.

25. Ibid. 287-289.

26. Ibid. VIII, 47, p. 566.

27. *Homélies pascales III*, p. 129.

28. Ibid. 129-131.

29. Pseudo-Cyprian, *De Pascha Computus* (PL 4:1028-1029); see C. Jones, *Bedae Opera de Temporibus* 12-13.

30. Hilarianus, *Expositum de die Paschae et Mensis* (PL 13:1107); see V. Loi, "Ilariano (Quinto Giulio)," *Dizionario patristico e di antichit' cristiane*, vol. 2 (Casale Monferrato 1984) 1746.

31. *Acta Synodi Caesariensis*, in *Studi e Testi* 59 (1933) 22.

32. Nicetas of Remesiana, *De Ratione Paschae*, in A. Burns, *Nicetas of Remesiana: His Life and Works* (Cambridge 1905) 98.

33. Cyril of Jerusalem, *Catechetical Lecture* XIV (PG 33:836): "As at the time when God created the sun and the moon, he gave equal course to the sun and the moon, so also some days ago at the time of the equinox."

34. Nicetas of Remesiana, *De Ratione Paschae* 98.

35. *Acta Synodi Caesariensis* 26.

36. The text is in *Neutestamentliche Apokryphen*, ed. W. Schneemelcher (Tübingen 1955) 334.

37. Epiphanius of Salamis, *Panarion*. Heresy 50, p. 245. In the west, churches in Gaul, according to Martin of Bracara, celebrated Easter on the fixed date of 25 March until the sixth century: "... sicut a plerisque gallicanis episcopis usque ante non multum tempus custoditum est." *De Pascha*, ed. A. Burns, *Nicetas of Remesiana, His Life and Works* 93. The *Acta Synodi Caesariensis* also reports: "Nam et omnes Gallii, quacumque die VIII Kalendas Aprilis fuisset, semper pascha celebrabant" (pp. 20-21).

38. T. Talley, *The Origins of the Liturgical Year* 12.

39. Q.J. Hilarian, Expositum de Die Paschae et Mensis, col. 1114; cf. *Homélies pascales III*, p. 127.

40. *Homélies pascales III*, p. 143.

41. Ibid. 131-141.

42. Ibid. 136.

43. Ibid. 145.

44. *De Paschate Iudaeorum* (PG 92:1133).

45. *Canon Paschalis* (PG 10:215).

46. Gregory of Nyssa, *Letter IV* (PG 46:1028).

Chapter Four
Easter and the Spring Full Moon

The Jewish Background

IN EARLY CHRISTIAN LITERATURE 14 NISAN, SOMETIMES CALLED ALSO THE "fourteenth of the month" or "fourteenth day of the moon," is identified with the day of the Easter full moon. This comes around the middle of the first Jewish month of Nisan. Consisting normally of twelve lunar months of twenty-nine and a half days each, the Jewish calendar is lunisolar, that is, the year is solar, while the months are lunar. In this particular system the spring full moon should always fall on 14 Nisan. Actually the moon rises on the evening of 14 Nisan, but since the day in the Jewish reckoning begins on the preceding evening, the full moon is said to rise on 15 Nisan or the night between the fourteenth and the fifteenth. Some early Christian writers had difficulty figuring out exactly what Jewish writers like Philo of Alexandria meant when they set the full moon on 15 instead of 14 Nisan.

The year, which comprises 365.25 solar days, exceeds in length the twelve lunar months by about eleven and a fourth days every year. Every three years or so this excess accumulates to as much as thirty-four days, so that the months no longer correspond to the natural seasons of the year, the equinoxes, and the solstices. If no measure is taken to synchronize them, it will happen every three years or so that 14 Nisan and hence the feast of Passover will occur a month earlier than the spring equinox. During the first three hundred years both the orthodox Jews and the official church impassionedly decried this anomaly. Ultimately the controversy between the Quartodecimans and those who kept Easter only on Sunday boiled down to this issue. In order to correct the anomaly it is necessary to intercalate in the lunar cycle of nineteen years a thirteenth month of thirty days, called the Second Adar (Adar is the twelfth month in the Jewish calendar). This is done on the third, sixth, eighth, eleventh, fourteenth, seventeenth, and nineteenth years. Intercalation is the normal device to synchronize the month of Nisan with spring and thus also the religious festivals with the appropriate seasons of the year. The system of intercalation was regarded as an act of compliance with the command of Exodus 13:10 that the feast of Passover should be kept "at its appointed time from year to year."

We can readily surmise the seriousness with which the Jews received this command. The *Book of Jubilees* assures them:

> No plague shall come upon them, if they observe Passover at its appointed time according to the ordinances. For the feast has been set on the appointed day, and no one may move it from one day to another or from one month to another. It must be observed at the proper time. Therefore command the children of Israel to keep the feast of Passover once a year on the appointed day.[1]

For the author of the book, who showed special preference for Tuesday, this is the apppointed day mentioned by Exodus 13:10. Obviously dissatisfied with the official calendar which assigned the feast of Easter to different days of the week, the author deviced a calendar in which 14 Nisan and hence Passover always fell on a Tuesday.[2]

In the prehistoric stage of Passover the full moon indicated to the shepherds the appropriate moment to hold the festival. With the adoption of the calendar, the feast had to be linked with a definite date in the calendar instead of the phase of the moon. Thus, 14 Nisan rather than the element of full moon became an article of liturgical legislation in Israel. Exodus 12:6 ordains that the paschal lamb chosen on the tenth day of Nisan shall be kept "until the fourteenth day of this month, and then, with the whole assembly of Israel present, it shall be slaughtered during the evening twilight." Likewise, Joshua 5:10, Leviticus 23:5, and Numbers 28:16 decree that "on the fourteenth day of the first month falls the Passover of the Lord." In patristic literature the fourteenth day of the first month or 14 Nisan and the day of the full moon are almost always used interchangeably.

We suggested early on that in the prehistoric Passover the full moon could have been a practical element of the nocturnal celebration, though we should not easily overlook its symbolism. In Jewish paschal theology the full moon took on a decidedly symbolic character. With penetrating insight Philo of Alexandria explored the symbolism of the full moon, leaving a cherished legacy to Christianity. In his book *The Special Laws* he writes:

> The feast begins at the middle of the month, on the fifteenth day, when the moon is full, a day purposely chosen, because then there is no darkness, but everything is continuously lighted up as the sun shines from the morning to the evening, and the moon from the evening to the morning, and while the stars give place to each other, no shadow is cast upon their brightness.[3]

We note in passing that some of the early Christian writers mistakenly attributed this phenomenon of continuous flood of light to the equinox, when the day and the night are of equal length. It is not very rare to find the spring equinox described in patristic literature as "the twenty-four hours of light," though Easter always falls after the equinox and sometimes a couple of days after the full moon.

Full Moon in Christian Tradition

A. Full Moon and the Easter Date

The element of the spring full moon was embedded in Easter theology and liturgy owing in large measure to the Quartodeciman observance. Whether or not this observance was of apostolic origin is a question which the Council of Nicea did not bother to ask. Although our information concerning the Quartodecimans before the year 125 is extremely fragmentary, it would not be precipitate to concede that there is at least some logic in their fervent claim that their observance came from the apostolic times. If we grant that the apostles commemorated the passover of Christ simultaneously as they were celebrating the Jewish Passover, we must conclude that they did so on 14 Nisan, following the Jewish calendar. It would be too difficult to think of any other day. Apropos Socrates, a fifth-century historian, writes:

> The Quartodecimans affirm that their observance of the fourteenth was handed down to them by the Apostle John. But the Romans and those in the West argue that the Apostles Paul

and Peter transmitted their existing practice to them. However, the two parties are not able to bring forward any written testimony to prove their assertion.[4]

St. Polycarp of Smyrna, himself a Quartodeciman, invoked the apostolic origin of the observance against the centralizing efforts of Pope Anicetus of Rome (d. 166) who wanted to enforce the practice of celebrating Easter exclusively on Sunday. When Pope Victor I (d. 199) issued letters of excommunication to the Quartodecimans of Asia for not observing the Easter Sunday canon, St. Irenaeus of Lyons urged him to moderation, reminding him that "in fact Anicetus could not persuade Polycarp to abandon the tradition which he had always observed with John, the disciple of the Lord, and the other Apostles with whom he lived."[5] Irenaeus added that "in his turn Polycarp did not persuade Anicetus to keep the Quartodeciman observance. He said that it was necessary for Anicetus to retain the practice of the bishops who preceded him." Polycrates, bishop of Ephesus and one of the leading Quartodeciman figures of the time, invoked the apostolicity of the observance in a pleading letter to Pope Victor. He named John, the disciple of the Lord, and Philip, "one of the twelve apostles," as sources of the observance. He also mentioned Polycarp of Smyrna, Thrasea of Eumenia, Sagaris of Laodicea, Papirius, Melito of Sardis, and his seven predecessors in Ephesus.[6]

The historian Socrates, who bitterly lamented the conduct of Pope Victor, made quite a stirring commentary on the controversy:

> Neither the Savior nor the apostles prescribed specific regulation concerning Easter. Neither the gospels nor the apostles threatened us with many punishments and imprecations. In Asia Minor there were many who neglected the Sabbath but observed nonetheless the fourteenth since ancient times. And though they did so, they were not considered separated from those who kept Easter on another day, until Victor, the bishop of Rome, greatly enraged, sent a letter of excommunication to the Quartodecimans in Asia.[7]

Eusebius of Caesarea did not advocate the Quartodeciman observance, but he respected it just the same as a "very ancient tradition." He wrote that some churches, "basing themselves on an apostolic tradition (*eks apostolikes paradóseos*), keep the usage which is in vigor until now."[8] The author of the *Chronicon Paschale*, on the other hand, struck a happy compromise when he claimed that after the ascension the apostles celebrated the death (*pascha*) of Christ on Friday, 14 Nisan, but on the following Sunday they celebrated his resurrection.[9]

In the west belief in the apostolic origin of the Quartodeciman observance was given credence at least by the year 450. The Irish Pseudo-Anatolius accepted the claim of the Quartodecimans that their tradition came from the Apostle John. He wrote:

> Until today all the bishops of Asia celebrate Easter every year without fail on the fourteenth day of the moon, after the equinox, when the Jews immolated the lamb. As a matter of fact they received this practice from an irreprehensible source, John the Evangelist, who leaned on the bosom of the Lord and without doubt drank from his spiritual doctrine.[10]

The author's report that even in his day all the bishops of Asia were Quartodecimans was surely a hearsay. We know that by the fifth century the observance was practically extinct in Asia, though it persisted in some places in Gaul until the sixth century. Pseudo-Anatolius acknowledged the apostolic origin of the Quartodeciman tradition, but he had no qualms in openly tagging it an act of disobedience to the bishops of Rome. He gently reprimanded the Quartodecimans for not acquiescing to the successors of the Apostles Peter and Paul, "who taught all the churches where they sowed the spiritual seed of the gospel, that the feast of the Lord's resurrection must be celebrated only on Sunday." But then, of course, the Quartodeciman Easter (*pascha*) centered more on the sacrifice of Christ on the cross than on the resurrection.

We meet two centuries later the spurious *Acta Synodi Caesariensis* which curiously affirmed that not only John but also all the other apostles celebrated Easter according to the Quartodeciman calendar. The writer explains that:

> after the ascension of our Savior the apostles were so engaged in preaching the Gospel, that they could not ordain anything regarding the Easter observance. Thus after they had been dispersed throughout the world, they celebrated Easter on whatever day in March on which the fourteenth day of the moon fell.[11]

This, he points out, is the reason why two different calendar traditions crept into the church after the death of the apostles. The Quartodecimans keep Easter on 14 Nisan "as they have seen it done by the Apostles." On the other hand, the discipline of fixing Easter on Sunday can be traced, according to him, to Pope Victor. This practice later made its way to the churches in Asia, through the instrumentality of Theophilus, bishop of Caesarea and Palestine, to whom Pope Victor delegated his authority "in order that all the catholic churches might celebrate the feast of Easter according to the correct canon."

The Quartodeciman trend to stress Easter as the celebration of Christ's passion was countered by those who regarded the paschal mystery as the totality of Christ's redeeming work. Although the western understanding of Easter tended to focus attention on Christ's resurrection, the mystery of his passion and death was never dissociated from the yearly celebration. The development of the Easter triduum which was extended to embrace the commemoration of the Lord's supper on Holy Thursday is sufficient evidence of this broader concept of Easter. We saw early on the artful attempt of Nicetas of Remesiana and the author of the *Acta Synodi Caesariensis* to include the passion and death of Christ in the Easter celebration. The stress on one or the other aspect of the paschal mystery might have given the impression of dichotomy or polarization, but the truth is neither of the camps denied the unity that exists between the death and the resurrection of Christ.

The author of the *Chronicon Paschale* realized the danger of underlining the resurrection to the detriment of the passion. He was distressed by people who scorned the church for its practice of calling Easter Sunday *pascha*. *Pascha*, according to the critics, referred to the death of Christ. Calling also the resurrection *pascha* showed ignorance. His answer consisted in affirming the unity of the paschal mystery: "It is necessary that the church give the name *pascha* not only to the passion and death of the Lord, but also to his resurrection."[12] We must concede that the word referred originally to the immolation of the paschal lambs at the full moon of spring and, among early Christians, also to the sacrifice of Christ on the cross. However, Christ's sacrifice did not end in death but in the resurrection, and we ourselves pass from death to life through the death and the resurrection of Christ. To press the point he expanded the pauline formula in 1 Corinthians 5:7 to read: "Christ our Passover has been sacrificed and has risen for us. Let us therefore call both the death and resurrection of the Lord *pascha*."[13]

The Quartodeciman *pascha* also implicitly contained the theme of the resurrection. But it gave to the passion and death of Christ such prominence, that his resurrection did not surface in the celebration. According to T. Talley, "there is little indication that the primitive Pascha was focused primarily on the resurrection, even though that theme was certainly included in the festival's celebration of our total redemption."[14] For the Quartodecimans the full moon on 14 Nisan was the decisive factor. It was the one element of the celebration that firmly laid hold of their Easter theology and spirituality. 14 Nisan showed, as no other cosmic element did, that the paschal victims in the Old Law had been replaced once and for all by the true paschal lamb who offered his life on the cross at the same time as these victims were being immolated in the temple. In a sense, 14 Nisan was witness to that event and now also a reminder of it. Deeply rooted in the johannine Easter theology, the Quartodecimans stubbornly defended the chronology which assigned the death of Christ on 14 Nisan.

Around the year 172 we meet an example of attachment to the 14-Nisan chronology that expressed itself almost to the point of belligerence. Apollinaris, bishop of Hierapolis in Phrygia, called to task those who

> feign that it was on the fourteenth day when the Lord ate the lamb with his disciples, and that it was on the feast of the unleavened bread [15 Nisan] when he suffered. And they explain according to their own interpretation what Matthew says. But in fact their explanation goes against God's law, for they make the gospels contradict each other.[15]

The 15-Nisan chronology, which was widespread as late as the fourth century outside the Quartodeciman camp, was actually part of Philo of Alexandria's legacy.[16] It will be remembered that he set the date of Passover on 15 Nisan, the day of the spring full moon. 15 Nisan obviously undermined the very foundation of the Quartodeciman *pascha*. Apollinaris fought against such error and formulated what should be regarded as the heart of the Quartodeciman theology: "The fourteenth day was the true passover of the Lord: the Son of God was the true sacrifice in place of the lambs."

The Easter homily which Melito of Sardis delivered around the year 170 is representative of the Quartodeciman theology which revolves around the typology of paschal lambs. On the basis of Exodus 12:2-6, which prescribes that the paschal lamb is to be separated from the herd on the tenth of the month and slaughtered on the fourteenth, Melito explains at length how the Old Testament figures which presaged the mystery of Christ have all been realized in his passover. He points out how Christ, the true lamb, was snatched from the company of his disciples also on the tenth and immolated toward evening on the fourteenth. Melito concludes his typological exposition by putting on the lips of Christ the solemn Quartodeciman tenet: "I am the passover of salvation; I am the lamb sacrificed for your sake."[17]

But this type of theology was not an exclusive domain of the Quartodecimans. It is in fact a combination of pauline and johannine typological reflections which are rather difficult to miss. One did not have to be a Quartodeciman to perceive the theological underpinning of the immolation of the paschal lambs. In his work *Dialogue with Trypho* St. Justin the Martyr (d. 165) provides us with an early example of this type of theological thinking.[18] In a point by point exposition of Old Testament prophecies he demonstrated to Trypho the Jew how these prophecies had all been fulfilled in and by Christ. At the time of the Exodus the blood of the *pascha* saved the Israelites from death. The event, said Justin, foreshadowed Christ's saving act in which he took the role of the victim. Like the paschal lambs he too was immolated on 14 Nisan.[19] Indeed, "Christ was the paschal lamb that was sacrificed, as Isaiah had foretold." Without hiding his sentiment of bitterness Justin reminded Trypho that "you seized him before the day of the Passover and crucified him on the day of the Passover."

The fervor with which the Quartodecimans defended their observance reveals a firm conviction of faith. 14 Nisan was a sure guarantee that their Easter theology would be perpetuated. It also signified the definitive substitution of the paschal lambs by Christ himself. This was what he meant to show when he died on the cross as the lambs were being sacrificed in the temple. And this was what the Quartodecimans proclaimed when they observed 14 Nisan faithfully. In contrast, the other group, while it recognized the symbolic value of the full moon, refused to celebrate the passover of Christ on any day but Sunday. For this group the relation of the full moon to Easter was purely practical in nature. The spring full moon served only as a clue to the correct reckoning of the Easter date. This explains in part the contradictory attitudes of admiration and hostility nursed by some early Christian writers toward the Easter full moon. Thus, it was among the Quartodecimans where 14 Nisan was considered an integral part of theology and a clear expression of faith. For it was on this day and on no other when the Son of God accomplished the work of redemption. With this frame of mind Polycrates could resolutely tell Pope Victor on behalf of his fellow Quartodecimans: "We observe the true and authentic day, neither adding to nor subtracting anything from it."[20]

The Quartodecimans linked Easter with the phase of the moon, not with the day of the week. There is something at once strange and familiar in this: strange, because when we speak of crucifixion we refer to a day, to Good Friday; familiar, because we too mark events in life according to the date of the month, regardless of the day of the week. Sometimes too we tend to associate certain events with cosmic manifestations like the full moon, sunset and twilight, raging storm, or violent earthquake. In times like these the day of the week fades into irrelevance. But more than anything else, the Quartodeciman observance sheds light on the church's sense of sacred time, on its consciousness of the temporal and cosmic dimension of salvation, and on its understanding of yearly anamnesis or anniversary of Christ's paschal mystery.

B. Sunday and the Easter Date

The Nicene canon requires three elements for the correct reckoning of the Easter date. These are the spring equinox, spring full moon, and Sunday. Although this canon runs into difficulties relative to the astronomical computation of 14 Nisan or the spring full moon, it is in fact quite easy to formulate. Easter is celebrated on Sunday after the full moon which rises after the spring equinox. There were some church Fathers who sensed divine intervention in this canon. Theophilus of Alexandria declared that it had been commanded by God, while the author of the *Chronicon Paschale* wrote that it was revealed by the Holy Spirit to the bishops at the Council of Nicea.[21] Such claims are, of course, both tenuous and tendentious. However, they represent the early church's pressing concern to break away from an anomalous Jewish calendar and to establish the supremacy of the Sunday observance.

The movement in favor of Sunday dates from the first quarter of the second century and became universal after the Council of Nicea, though it would appear that the council was more immediately concerned with the question of the spring equinox. The movement consisted of two stages which should be neatly distinguished. The first stage, which is the core of the observance, obliged all the churches not to celebrate Easter except on Sunday. The second stage went farther and forbade the celebration of Easter even on Sunday, should this fall on the full moon. Clearly the chief intentions behind the second prohibition were: first, to effect a total rupture with the Jewish Passover and second, to forestall a relapse into the observance of 14 Nisan on the part of ex-Quartodecimans. The bottom line was not to celebrate with the Jews at all, so much so that if Sunday fell on the full moon, Easter had to be postponed to the following Sunday.

This was an extreme measure which the author of the *Chronicon Paschale* translated into a binding Easter canon: "If the fourteenth falls on Sunday, we the disciples of the catholic church of Christ celebrate Easter on the following Sunday in order not to celebrate at the same time as the Jews."[22] While it is historically certain that the Council of Nicea fixed Easter Sunday after the passing of the spring equinox, there is no solid proof that it censured the celebration of Easter Sunday on the day of the full moon. This seems to be a post-conciliar development which started in Alexandria whence it spread to the other churches. Before Rome accepted the Alexandrian upper limit of 25 April, there must have been occasions when it was in a quandary whether to celebrate after its upper limit of 21 April or on the day of the full moon. In 387, a memorable year in the history of the controversy over the Easter date, Rome apparently celebrated Easter Sunday on 18 April which was the day of the full moon or, in other words, on the same day as the Jews.

There was an adjoining motive for supporting the practice of celebrating Easter after the full moon. It involved, or so the church Fathers thought, the question of the Easter fast.[23] Originally a three-day ascetical preparation for the reception of baptism at Easter Vigil, fasting eventually came to be regarded as a form of participation in the passion of the Lord.[24] Hence, it was not to be broken until after the full moon, for Christ died when it was full moon. If the full moon fell on Sunday, then the Easter fast had to be broken a day earlier. Only the Manicheans fasted on Sunday, a vile and degenerate practice which, according to St. Ambrose, amounted to outright denial of the resurrection of Christ.[25] But if because of Sunday the fast is broken, the venerable discipline of fasting for three complete days until the full moon would not be properly complied with. The alternative was to move Easter to the following week, so that the triduum of fasting could be fully observed until after the Easter Vigil.

Theophilus of Alexandria explains that Easter Sunday is postponed to the following week, "lest we break the fast on Saturday which is only the thirteenth day of the moon," that is, the day before the Lord's passion and death.[26] Likewise the author of the *Chronicon Paschale* maintains that fasting should not be broken on Saturday, 13 Nisan, because Christ died on 14 Nisan. On the other hand, fasting may not be continued until 14 Nisan, if this should fall on Sunday.[27] Hence, for the sake of the triduum of Easter fast it became necessary to move Easter to the week after 14 Nisan.

St. Ambrose of Milan addressed the issue in a letter to the bishops of Aemilia in 386. He prefaced his thinking with the principle that if the Easter full moon falls on Sunday, "the feast of Easter is to be put off to the following week, because we may not fast on Sunday nor may we break it on Saturday, the thirteenth of the moon, since fasting is observed most especially on the day of the passion."[28] The difficulty which the contemporaries of Ambrose saw in this was how to justify the distance of one week between Easter Sunday and the full moon. Ambrose gibed them for their useless preoccupation to coordinate Easter with the phases of the moon. To press his point he brought to their attention the classic case of the following year. In that year 15 Nisan, the day of Christ's passion, would fall on Monday; 16 Nisan, the day of his burial, would fall on Tuesday; and 17 Nisan, the day of his resurrection, would fall on Wednesday. If we followed the phases of the moon, we would have to celebrate Easter on Wednesday!

In the same letter Ambrose assigned the death of Christ to 14 Nisan, the day when strict fasting should be observed. "Hence, we should obey the Easter canon, namely that we do not keep the fourteenth as the day of the resurrection, but rather as the day of the passion."[29] Did Christ then die on the fourteenth or the fifteenth? The tenor of Ambrose's letter indicates that this particular question did not quite interest him. What mattered in the final analysis was not 14 or 15 Nisan, but the discipline of not fasting on Sunday and of not cutting short the traditional three days of fasting. What Ambrose did not explain is that the discipline actually boiled down to the post-Nicene canon which had so severed Easter from the Jewish Passover, that a simultaneous celebration even on Sunday was interdicted. But apart from this consideration, Ambrose has the distinction of having underplayed, against existing tradition, the role of the spring full moon in the computation of the Easter date.

Full moon or 14 Nisan suffered another blow when some writers tried to extend it for seven days, that is, until 21 Nisan. This means that any day within this period of time could be considered 14 Nisan! In short, its role in the computation of Easter had become plainly subsidiary. Sunday held the primacy. Such machination was clearly dictated by a need to soothe the scruples of those who, having abandoned 14 Nisan, still felt some attachment to or respect for the prescription of Exodus 12 regarding 14 Nisan. For it is quite understandable that the ordinary faithful, after hearing this biblical passage, would have wondered why the church did not observe it. The answer they received was that the church, in its own way, still observed the Mosaic regulation regarding 14 Nisan. One writer explained that the Jews considered the seven days of Unleavened Bread still part of the Passover feast. Thus there was really nothing amiss when the church celebrated Easter on one of those seven days. Another writer argued that if the Mosaic Law permitted a second Passover in the second month, why should the church not be allowed to celebrate Easter a week after 14 Nisan? A third writer reasoned that if ten contained nine, then surely 21 Nisan contained 14 Nisan![30]

A closely related question was in connection with the light of the full moon. When the Council of Nicea linked Easter with the day of the week rather than the phase of the moon, the feast sometimes fell several days after the full moon, so that it appeared like the feast of the waning moon. In fact, Easter Vigil homilies paid little attention to the full moon. Some stopped at the light of paschal candles and lamps which substituted for the missing moonlight. But the question here was of a theoretical character. The writer of the *Canon Paschalis* considered it a matter of principle that Easter ought to be celebrated when there was maximum light, "for the feast of the Lord's resurrection is light, and light has no fellowship with darkness."[31] That is why, the absence of the full moon at the Easter Vigil was in itself something to be deplored, especially when Easter Sunday had to be postponed for an entire week. But we receive the consoling assurance from the author that even then the moon still "illumines the greater part of the night, as it rises at the second watch." In other words, as long as Easter Sunday did not fall beyond 21 Nisan, it would still enjoy more light than darkness.[32]

The underlying reason for the seven-day extension of 14 Nisan was, therefore, the canon which fixed Easter on Sunday. No sacrifice was too great, not even the light of the full moon which originally not only marked the moment of the nocturnal feast but also graphically portrayed the fullness of life the celebrants longed for. A good number of early Christian writers solemnly declared that Christ died on 14 Nisan, but as soon as Sunday was involved all they did was pay lip service to the full moon. As the author of *Chronicon Paschale* candidly admits, 14 Nisan had to be extended for seven days on account of Sunday (*diá ten tes kyriakès hemèran*).[33]

We see a certain order of precedence among the elements constituting the Easter date, namely Sunday, full moon, and equinox. Nicetas of Remesiana develops both the spiritual and theological reasons for such order of precedence:

> Our elders prudently fixed the date of Easter relative to the moon and the week rather than the equinox. For the full moon illumines the dark night, in the same way as the light of the Spirit frees us from the corruption of darkness. Besides, after the equinox Easter is celebrated in greater light and within a shorter night. Our elders preferred to link the feast with the day than with the moon, when both cannot be observed. They chose to disregard the fourteenth day of the moon instead of Sunday, because our salvation is in the resurrection.[34]

Notwithstanding the state of insignificance to which the full moon had practically been reduced, it continued to hold a certain mystique among the church Fathers and to play a decisive role in the reckoning of the Easter date. Thus, the relationship between Sunday and the full moon lingered on in the thoughts of the Fathers. One exception was Cyril of Alexandria who scorned the full moon as the symbol of the devil, calling it the "bastard light" in the night.[35] In his first Easter letter he writes: "For justice to arise, it is necessary that the moon be removed, for the moon is the symbol of the devil, the prince of the night."[36]

The Symbolism of the Easter Full Moon

One of the finest homilies dealing with the symbolism of the Easter full moon was written by St. Gregory of Nyssa.[37] The homily was occasioned by a carping observation of the Jews on the half-hearted compliance of the church with the Mosaic paschal regulations: "If you observe the fourteenth, then eat the prescribed meal. If you do not observe the fourteenth, why waste your energy on computing the correct day of the feast?" It is curious that the Jews, at least according to Gregory's report, had the impression that Christians observed 14 Nisan. It is possible that they had in mind the small Quartodeciman communities that were still extant in the fourth century. But the criticism could have been directed against others who, in their particular way, took 14 Nisan into account when they computed the date of Easter Sunday. Gregory answered that the Mosaic regulations have value only when they can cleanse a person from sins. The Sabbath rest signifies cessation from evil work; circumcision, the removal of lust; and unleavened bread, purity of life, that is, a life without the admixture of the old ferment of vice. 14 Nisan has meaning for Christians in so far as it symbolizes renewal of life.

Gregory developed in the same homily the Easter theme of continuous light inspired by the natural phenomenon of twenty-four hours of uninterrupted light. The theme was first brought to attention by Philo of Alexandria from whom it was borrowed gratefully by several Christian writers who turned it into an impressive element of Easter spirituality. Gregory prefaced his spiritual reflection with a description of the phenomenon that looks like an expanded version of Philo's:

> Before the rays of the sun totally disappear, the moon rises on the other horizon to shed its light on the world. Before the moon completes its night journey, the brightness of the sun already mingles with the moon's remaining light. Darkness is thus completely absent on the night of the full moon because of the uninterrupted succession of the sun and the moon.[38]

This natural phenomenon, according to Gregory, "is a symbol for those who celebrate spiritually throughout the entire week of life, so that every day of their life they may celebrate one bright and shadowless Easter."[39]

The Easter full moon symbolizes the quality of Christian life, a life lived fully in the light, without the mixture of darkness. Gregory presents the Easter week as compendium of the entire life of Christians. In this week their entire life is, as it were, contained in a symbol. The week-long celebration is a reminder to Christians that they should live their lives in the brightness of Christ's resurrection. Christian life should thus be regarded as an endless Easter feast. In Gregory's own words, "we keep the fourteenth, in order that we may perceive from the light received by the senses the other light which is understood by the mind alone. While we keep the law regarding the full moon, let us realize that the law was given for no other reason than to urge us to spend all the days of our life illumined by virtues and free from the work of darkness."[40]

Theophilus of Alexandria also developed in his *Prologue to Easter Letters* the theme of light provided by the Easter full moon. "The Law," he writes, "prescribes that Easter should be held on the fourteenth of the first month, so that by imitating the light of the full moon we, who possess the full light of the mind, may dwell far away from the darkness of sin."[41] While the keyword in Gregory of Nyssa's reflection is *symbolon*, in Theophilus' it is *mímema* or imitation. The spring full moon signifies fullness, perfection, and abundance. Christians are called to imitate it. The people of antiquity ascribed the growth of plants, animals, and all living things to the action of the moon. Theophilus saw in the spring full moon an exemplar, a model, for Christians to imitate. Christians should grow in the fullness of virtue, free from the darkness of sin, and abundant in good work.

Western writers also addressed the theme of light. St. Ambrose of Milan explains that "the passover of the Lord is celebrated on the fourteenth day of the moon, because those who celebrate Easter ought to be perfect, ought to love the Lord Jesus who in his love for his people gave himself up to suffering with perfect love."[42] The full moon is the symbol of perfection. For Ambrose the perfection of love expresses itself in self-giving, in sacrifice for others unto death. That is why, he calls number 14 *grande numeri mysterium*, the symbol of the Father's love for us: "For it was on the fourteenth, when the moon was brightly shining, that the Father handed his only Son to death for our sake."[43] The words of St. Jerome echo the same doctrine:

We read in the Book of Exodus that the lamb is immolated on the fourteenth day of the month. It is immolated on the fourteenth when the moon is full, when nothing is lacking in its brightness. Thus you see that Christ was not immolated except in perfect and full light.[44]

This early Christian reflection on 14 Nisan or the Easter full moon invites us to take a more penetrating look at this much controverted element of the Easter date. It is ironic that the Fathers who discarded 14 Nisan from their system of computing the Easter date were those who were most eloquent in exalting its worth, so powerful must have been its mystique. We are given the impression that Easter always falls on 14 Nisan. And if we accept the odd system of extending 14 Nisan up to seven days, then indeed Easter always falls, at least theoretically, on the day of the full moon, even if in reality the moon is already waning. But we should not seek the meaning of the Easter full moon exclusively in its natural symbolism. Ultimately its meaning rests on its being a component of the date of Easter. If it had not been for this, the early Christian writers would probably have simply ignored it. In fact, when it did not serve their purpose, some of them maligned it. In its role of date the full moon brings us back to the time when Christ fulfilled the prophetic figure of the paschal lamb slain and immolated for the redemption of God's people.

We need not lament the waning importance of the moon in our Easter celebrations. For Christianity the doctrine of the resurrection is the heart of faith: it alone can shed light on the ultimate meaning of life, of world events, and of human history. Nothing is, therefore, more logical than to heighten its value in the life of people. This necessarily leads to the appreciation of Sunday as the day of the resurrection. We should, of course, avoid any dichotomy between the death and resurrection of Christ. The early Christian authors themselves, though they stressed the glory of the risen Lord, were deeply aware of the unity among the various aspects of the paschal mystery.

At some time in history Sunday might have unfortunately understated the value of the prophetic fulfillment that the full moon represents, but it has certainly endowed the Christian version of Passover with a sense of finality, the resurrection.

NOTES

1. The text is in E. Littman, *Die Apokryphen und Pseudepigraphen des Alten Testaments* (Tübingen 1900) 15.

2. J. Van Goudoever: *Biblical Calendars* (Leiden 1961) 63.

3. Philo of Alexandria, *The Special Laws* II (Massachusetts 1958) 401.

4. Socrates, *History of the Church* V, 22 (PG 67:632). See T. Talley, *The Origins of the Liturgical Year* (New York 1986) 5-27. A fourth-century Quartodeciman, Terentius, wrote to Peter of Alexandria in defense of the observance: "We have no other purpose than to keep the memory of his passion at the time which has been handed down to us by its witnesses, even before the Egyptians [Alexandrians] received the faith" (PG 18:517).

5. The text is in Eusebius, *History of the Church* V, Sources chrétiennes, vol. 41 (1955) 71.

6. See *Fragments on Easter* (PG 5:1357-1361). Epiphanius of Salamis (*Panarion*, Heresy 70) also reports on the controversy, but he mistakes Polycrates for Polycarp, and thus pairs Victor with Polycarp; see also Sozomen's *History of the Church* VII, 19.

7. Socrates, *History of the Church* V, 22, col. 628.

8. Eusebius of Caesarea, *History of the Church* V, p. 71.

9. *Chronicon Paschale* (PG 92:548). See B. Botte, "La question pascale: pâque du vendredi ou pâque du dimanche?," *La Maison-Dieu* 41 (1955) 84-95.

10. Pseudo-Anatolius, *Canon Paschalis* (PG 10:217).

11. Ibid. 607.

12. *Chronicon Paschale* (PG 92:549).

13. Ibid.

14. T. Talley, *The Origins of the Liturgical Year* 5; see "Pâque," *Dictionnaire d'archéologie chrétienne et de liturgie*, vol. 13, 2, p. 1524.

15. The text is in O. Perler, *Méliton de Sardes, Sur la Pâque et Fragment*, Sources chrétiennes, vol. 123 (1966) 244.

16. The chronology which assigns the death of Christ on 15 Nisan was held by Eusebius of Caesarea: *On Holy Easter* (PG 29:705); Proterius of Alexandria, *Letter to Pope Leo* (PL 67:509); Eutychius of Constantinople, *On Easter and the Holy Eucharist* (PG 87:2397); Pseudo-Cyprian, *De Pascha Computus* (PL 4:1046); and Ambrose of Milan, *Epistola XXIII* (PL 16:1074).

17. Melito of Sardis, *On Easter*, Sources chrétiennes, vol. 123 (1966) 122.

18. Justin the Martyr, *Dialogue with Trypho* CXI, 3, *Textes et Documents* (Paris 1909) 170-172.

19. Other church Fathers outside the Quartodeciman camp who accepted 14 Nisan as the date of Christ's death were: Hippolytus of Rome (*Fragments of Easter Homilies* [PG 10:869]) and Clement of Alexandria (*Chronicon Paschale* [PG 92:81]).

20. The text is in Eusebius of Caesarea, *History of the Church*, V, 24, p. 68.

21. Theophilus of Alexandria, *Prologue to Easter Letters* (PG 65:48); *Chronicon Paschale* (PG 92:84).

22. *Chronicon Paschale* (PG 92:548).

23. See R. Cabié, "Christian Initiation," in *The Church at Prayer*, vol. 3 (Collegeville 1988) 33-34; see T. Talley's informative treatment of the Easter fast in the early church in *The Origins of the Liturgical Year* 27-31.

24. Hippolytus of Rome imposed fasting on candidates for baptism from Friday to the Vigil; see *Apostolic Tradition*, ed. B. Botte (Münster 1963) 42.

25. Ambrose of Milan, *Epistola XXIII* (PL 16:1073). Theophilus of Alexandria also condemned the practice; see *Prologue to Easter Letters* (PG 65:51).

26. Theophilus of Alexandria, *Prologue to Easter Letters* (PG 65:49-51).

27. *Chronicon Paschale* (PG 92:97-100).

28. Ambrose of Milan, *Epistola XXIII* (PL 16:1073)

29. Ibid. 1073; cf. 1071 and 1074.

30. Gaudentius of Brescia taught that the extension of 14 Nisan was ordained by God; see *Tractatus I in Exodum*, *Tractatus Paschales*, Corpus Scriptorum Ecclesiasticorum Latinorum, vol. 68 (1936) 20.

31. *Canon Paschalis* (PG 10:215).

32. Ibid.; cf. Nicetas of Remesiana, *De Ratione Paschae* 106.

33. *Chronicon Paschale* (PG 92:549).

34. Nicetas of Remesiana, *De Ratione Paschae* 105-106; see Hilarian, *Expositum de Die Paschae et Mensis* (PL 13:1114). Hilarian speaks of the primacy of Sunday over the first month and the full moon "ad instar resurrectionis."

35. Cyril of Alexandria, *Glaphyra in Exodum* (PG 59:424).

36. Cyril of Alexandria, *Easter Letter* I (PG 77:408). Epiphanius of Salamis preferred the symbolism of the spring sun to the moon, because when Christ died on 14 Nisan, the moon began to wane; see *Against Heresies* (PG 41:885).

37. Gregory of Nyssa, *On Easter* I (*PG* 46:617-619); cf. Philo of Alexandria, *The Special Laws* II (Massachusetts 1958) 401.

38. Ibid. 621.

39. Ibid.

40. Ibid.

41. Theophilus of Alexandria, *Prologue to Easter Letters* (PG 65:49).

42. Ambrose of Milan, *De Obitu Theodosii*, Corpus Scriptorum Ecclesiasticorum Latinorum, vol. 73 (1955) 391.

43. Ibid.

44. Jerome, *Tractatus de Psalmo XIV in Quadragesima*, Corpus Christianorum Latinorum, vol. 78 (1958) 30; see also *De Exodo, In Vigilia Paschae*, ibid. 536.

Chapter Five
The Evening Hours of Easter

UNLIKE SPRING, EQUINOX, AND THE FULL MOON, EVENING IS AN ELEMENT OF THE Easter date that left no conspicuous imprint on Christian liturgy. If not for the afternoon celebration on Good Friday, which corresponds to Matthew 27:46's narrative that Christ died toward midafternoon, this Easter element would have been a mere anecdote. But if liturgy neglected it, patristic literature searched deeply into its symbolism and spiritual meaning.

Exodus 12:6 prescribes that the paschal lamb procured for sacrifice on 10 Nisan should be kept until 14 Nisan, "and then with the whole assembly of Israel present, it shall be slaughtered during the evening twilight."[1] Evening twilight in this legislation was interpreted in two ways. The Samaritans understood it as the time between sunset and the setting in of darkness. The Pharisees and the Talmud, on the other hand, understood it as the intervening hours between afternoon and dusk. The latter interpretation set the date for the immolation of the lambs on 14 Nisan itself, that is, before sunset. The paschal meal, however, had to be eaten in the evening or at night, that is, during the first hours of 15 Nisan. In the context of this tradition the preparatory ritual of slaughtering the paschal lambs can be considered part of the feast of Passover, although the meal was eaten only after sunset.

The church Fathers caught a gleam of allegorical meaning in evening twilight. The paschal lamb slain in the evening and whose blood saved the Israelites from the angel of death was the figure of Christ. For he too was sacrificed for our sake and we, like the Israelites, have been marked with his blood against the power of sin.

The fact that Christ died at that hour when the lambs were being slain opened a new horizon in Easter theology.[2] The hour of Christ's death impressed on the consciousness of early Christian writers the eschatological dimension of his paschal sacrifice. The immolation of the paschal lambs toward evening did much to sharpen this consciousness. Christ's death took place in the evening of created time and thereby transported the world to its final stage, the last *aíon*.

Thus in patristic literature dealing with Easter typology the evening hours transcend the confines of temporal existence. It points to the eschatological era, the end of the world, the age in which God's promise of salvation which had been foreshadowed by the sacrifice of the paschal lambs is brought to fulfillment by the sacrifice of the Lamb of God. It is probable that this typology was influenced by the Easter catechesis of 1 Peter 1:18-20, which speaks of "these last days" when the blood of the spotless, unblemished lamb was revealed for our sake.[3] It is not clear whether this passage had in mind the evening of Passover as point of reference, but for the early Christian writers there was no question that the evening of Passover refers to the evening of this present age.

Origen was one of the first to broach the eschatological meaning of the evening hours. Reproaching those who still followed the Jewish paschal regulations, he declared that "God detests those who think that the feast of the Lord is confined to a single day," that Easter is celebrated only once a year.[4] Everyday is the feast of Easter, because everyday we Christians eat the flesh of the Word, the *Verbi caro*, the flesh of Christ our Passover who was immolated for us. We are quite sure that Origen did not mean a daily eucharistic celebration, which was still unknown in the third century.[5] But he could have referred to a daily rite of communion at home or to the reading of Scripture.[6] Later in the fourth century the connection between Easter and a daily eucharistic celebration would take shape in the thinking of St. Augustine. In an Easter homily Augustine encouraged the faithful to participate daily in the Easter celebration "in which we share daily at the table of his body and blood."[7] Eusebius of Caesarea, on the other hand, would speak of a weekly Easter:

> We who belong to the New Testament and who celebrate his passover every Sunday are always nourished by the body of the Savior and share in the blood of the lamb. We keep the feast of Easter by celebrating the mysteries every week on the day of the Savior.[8]

The point we wish to pursue is whether Origen, Eusebius, and Augustine, among others who regarded the present time as the final phase of salvation history, saw some connection between the Lord's supper and the evening hours of Easter. If so, they must have perceived an eschatological dimension in the eucharistic celebration. The eucharist does not only recall in anamnesis the Lord's supper and sacrifice, it also transports the world to the evening of time. Whenever we celebrate the eucharist, we proclaim that the Lord is about to return and that in the final analysis there is nothing else to look forward to but the coming of a new heaven and a new earth. For these considerations alone we can rightly speak of the eucharist as the celebration par excellence of the period between Christ's death and his second coming. The eucharist is the identifying and distinguishing mark of the present dispensation.

But how does the feast of Easter relate to the evening of time? Origen writes: "Because the law of Passover requires that the lamb be eaten in the evening, the Lord suffered in the evening of the world, so that you who are in the evening until morning dawns may always eat the flesh of the Word."[9] In another passage Origen says: "We are commanded to sacrifice the lamb toward evening, because the Savior, who is our true lamb, came into this world at the last hour (*eschâte hóra*)."[10] In short, by virtue of Christ's paschal sacrifice the world entered into the evening of its existence, into the eschatological era. Origen notes, however, that evening and eschatology should not convey the sentiment of gloom or drive us into despair. Rather, they indicate a time of continuous feasting, because Christ our Passover has been immolated. For Christians life is like an evening of festivity that reflects the endless feast of the kingdom.[11]

Origen develops this idea in an homily where he explained the symbolism of number 10 in connection with 10 Nisan.[12] He saw meaning in the fact that both the preparation for the feast of the Passover and the entry of the Israelites into the promised land took place on the tenth day of the first month. The mystery of number 10, he explains, teaches that we too are invited to celebrate our passover and summoned to enter into the promised land, that is, the bliss of perfection. Such bliss is not something which we shall experience only in the world to come: in fact it has already commenced. The eschatological age is here. It is God's *hodie* or the reality of "today," indicating the presence of salvation in our day-to-day existence. Since Christ has completed his work of redemption, our "today" signifies the end of the ages, the evening of time, which stands at the threshold of the future kingdom. That kingdom will be ours "tomorrow, that is, after the consummation of the world."[13] Our final deliverance flashes on the horizon, assuring us that it is near at hand.

Gregory of Nazianzus echoes the thoughts of Origen about the meaning of evening. He too interprets the evening when Christ suffered as the consummation of the ages (*syntéleia ton aiónon*).[14] But he moves on to develop the idea of the *triton pascha* or the three stages of Easter, a celebrated patristic theme which later writers used to great spiritual advantage. The first stage, according to Gregory, was a prophetic figure, the second was its reality, and the third will be its perfection. The Jewish Passover was the figure or image of our Easter. This in turn is but a figure of the third and final Easter, the eternal feast which we shall celebrate in the kingdom. Gregory, a theologian and pastor of deep Easter spirituality, lived his life in expectation of the hour when the third stage of Easter would finally unfold itself. In a moving farewell letter he wrote toward the end of his life, he revealed his burning desire to pass from the Egypt of this present world, in order to celebrate the eternal Easter in the company of all the saints.[15]

The symbolic character of evening received greater theological depth in the work of an unknown writer whom history simply names Pseudo-Chrysostom.[16] The author is meticulous in his consideration of details. He observes that the lamb had to be immolated not in the evening but toward evening (*pròs hespéran*). That is why, Christ suffered and died not at the end but toward the end of time or, in the language of theology, the eschatological age. In the context of salvation history this comes as the final stage in the series of divine interventions in the life of his people. The first stage, symbolized by 10 Nisan, embraces the period time from Adam to Noah; the second (11 Nisan) from Noah to Abraham; the third (12 Nisan) from Abraham to Moses; the fourth (13 Nisan) from Moses to the advent of Christ; and the fifth (14 Nisan) from the sacrifice of Christ to his return on the last day.

Pseudo-Chrysostom notes further that the paschal lambs were chosen on 10 Nisan, the day when, according to him, the first parents were created. He perceives a hidden meaning in this. It tells us that we can catch a glimpse of the sacrifice of Christ, the Lamb of God, already in the story of creation. When God created the first parents, he pointed to their and their progeny's redemption through the blood of his Son. Furthermore, the assignation of the patriarchs to the various stages of salvation history suggests that there is continuity in God's plan from the moment of creation up to the coming of Christ. It suggests too that the sacrifice of Christ is the culminating point in the long series of God's dealings with his people. That is why, Christ did not suffer until the fourteenth day, toward evening, that is, at the close of the ages. The doctrine is strongly evocative of 1 Peter 1:19-20, which sings of the lamb that was "chosen before the world's foundation," but was "revealed for your sake in these last days."[17]

Latin writers also explored the relationship between the evening hours of Easter and eschatology. Like the Greeks, they approached the subject from the perspective of biblical typology. The earliest record we possess comes from the year 243. The African Pseudo-Cyprian, author of the renowned *De Pascha Computus*, reads in the light of Christ's mystery all the instructions God gave to the Israelites concerning the Passover celebration: the first month, the full moon, the manner of preparing the paschal meal, and the ritual to be observed when eating the meal. Ironically the crime committed by the Jews against Christ was concealed under the veneer of observing the Passover prescriptions. For "those who had been held in Egypt came out toward evening, that is, toward the end of time, their loins girded and sandals on their feet, in order to seize the immaculate Lamb of God with swords and sticks. And they did to him all the things which had been foretold by the prophets."[18] Pseudo-Cyprian calls the sin committed by the Jews *latrocinium*. They had been forewarned about it since the beginning of the world, *ab initio saeculi*. For Pseudo-Cyprian the beginning of the world refers, surprisingly, not to the creation of the world but to the Passover in Egypt. His Easter typology goes only as far back as the Egyptian Passover.

St. Jerome also developed the theme of Easter evening in his celebrated Easter Vigil homily on the exodus.[19] Today, he said, the Israelites leave Egypt. Today the Lamb of God who takes away the sin of the world is sacrificed for the salvation of all. Today the posts of our houses, that is, our foreheads, are marked with the blood of the lamb. Today the Egyptians are killed and the people of God are freed from the servitude of Pharaoh. What the Israelites experienced in figure the true people of God experience today in reality. Jerome explains the meaning of the word "today." It signifies the evening of the present world. It means that the Lamb of God was immolated not during the day but toward evening, or in his own words, "our Lord and Savior suffered at the close of the ages."

Easter is the exodus of Christians. But Jerome holds no illusions. He knows that there are people who, although already freed, prefer to remain slaves of sin. He tells his listeners: "John in his letter says that now is the last hour. At the last hour, when the day is over, night falls. By this we are made to understand that as long as we remain in Egypt, we are not in the light but in darkness." The exodus produces tension in our lives as Christians. Today we leave Egypt, and the fetters of our slavery are broken; yet we still dwell in the land of Egypt, we still labor in darkness. We shine like the moon in the night, but it is still night and we do not possess fully the splendor of the true Sun. This is the type of paradox we meet in an Easter homily of Eusebius of Caesarea: "We are always departing from Egypt, we are always crossing the desert of human life, we always tend toward God, we always celebrate Easter."[20]   Christian life is a continual struggle against darkness, and that is what our daily, weekly, and yearly celebration of Easter signifies.

Another western writer who dealt at length with the symbolism of the Easter evening was St. Gaudentius of Brescia. In one of his treatises on the exodus he notes that Christ "was taken prisoner on the tenth day of the first month and sacrificed by the Jews on the fourteenth day toward the evening of the present world."[21] It will be remembered that according to the Quartodeciman passion chronology Christ, like the paschal lamb, was seized on the tenth and was held prisoner by the priests until the fourteenth. In the typology of Gaudentius 10 symbolizes the decalogue of the Mosaic Law into which Christ, by becoming a man, was received by the Jews. For, as Galatians 4:4 tells us, "when the designated time had come, God sent forth his Son born of a woman, born under the law." He was born fourteen generations after the Babylonian captivity, which is the last of all the generations in the genealogy of Matthew 1:2-16. And he was crucified toward the evening of the fourteenth. The evening hours of Easter are thus the symbol of the "evening of this world, for Christ suffered when the world came to its final hour." It was probably to underline the extraordinary nature of the evening of Christ's death that Gaudentius speaks of it as a "miracle." It was not a normal evening; it was rather premature darkness, "for when the Lord was crucified, the sun set at midday."[22]

The foregoing patristic reflections on the evening hours of Easter unveil the eschatological character of Christ's death. They tell us that the sacrifice of the Lamb of God was the culminating point of God's series of interventions in human history. The Messiah has come: God's plan of salvation has been realized; there will be no new messiahs and no new plans. The sacrifice of Christ took place in the evening to signify that when he fulfilled the promise of salvation, he brought the existence of the world and the course of human events to their conclusion. The world has reached its evening twilight. It is in a phase of transition. When at last the darkness shall have ended, the world will be bathed in the light of the eternal day.

We discover in these reflections a healthy and consoling sense of finality in God's plan of salvation. They lead us to believe in the depths of our consciousness that both cosmic and human existence can no longer be satisfactorily explained apart from the death of Christ. At the same time they make us realize that life is a steady movement toward the eschatological evening, toward the fulfillment of God's plan for the world and each one of us. Finally, they assure us that salvation is already present in our midst. We are able to have a foretaste, while still in the evening hours of this world, of the glory of the resurrection. It means that while we push on in search of the eternal kingdom, we in fact already dwell in the reality of its earthly shadow.

NOTES

1. See also Lv 23:5, Dt 16:5-6, Nm 28:16, and Jos 5:10.

2. S. Marsili, "La liturgia attuazione del mistero pasquale," in *Anamnesis*, vol. 1 (Casale Monferrato 1988) 96-100.

3. M.-E. Boismard, "Une liturgie baptismale dans la Prima Petri," *Revue bénédictine* (1965) 183-90.

4. Origen, *In Genesim Homiliae X*, 3, Sources chrétiennes, vol. 7 (1947) 189; see also *Contra Celsum* VIII, 22 (PG 10:1552): "Is etiam, qui cogitat Christum, quod pascha nostrum est, immolatum esse et manducanda Verbi carne festum diem agi oportere, semper Pascha, quod transitum significat, celebrat."

5. See R. Taft's study, "The Frequency of the Eucharist throughout History," *Beyond East and West: Problems in Liturgical Understanding* (Washington, D.C. 1984) 61-80.

6. For Origen the expression *Verbi caro* means either the *munus consecratum* or eucharist (cf. *Homilia in Exodum* 13, 3) or the word of God in Scripture (cf. *Homilia in Numerum* 16, 9).

7. Augustine of Hippo, *Wilmart IX de S. Pascha* II (PL: Suppl. II:724-725).

8. Eusebius of Caesarea, *On the Feast of Easter* (PG 24:701).

9. Origen, *In Genesim Homiliae X*, 3, Sources chrétiennes, vol. 7 (1947) 189.

10. Origen, *Selecta ad Exodum* (PG 12:284).

11. Origen, *In Leviticum Homiliae* XIII (PG 12:546).

12. Origen, *In Iosue Homiliae*, Sources chrétiennes, vol. 71 (1960) 132.

13. Ibid. 326-328.

14. Gregory of Nazianzus, *On Holy Easter* II (PG 36:644).

15. Gregory of Nazianzus, *Letter to Helladius* (PG 37:216).

16. The text is in *Homélies Pascales* II, ed. P. Nautin, Sources chrétiennes, vol. 36 (1953) 63.

17. For the author of the *Chronicon Paschale*, the sixth day, when the first parents were created, was also the day when Christ died on the cross, thereby signifiying that the sixth day is the advent of the consummation of the world (PG 92:541).

18. *De Pascha Computus* (PL 4:1026-1027).

19. Jerome, *De Exodo. In Vigilia Paschae*, Corpus Christianorum Latinorum, vol. 2 (1958) 536-537.

20. Eusebius of Caesarea, *On the Feast of Easter* (PG 24:701).

21. Gaudentius of Brescia, *Tractatus III in Exodum, Tractatus Paschales*, Corpus Scriptorum Ecclesiasticorum Latinorum, vol. 68 (1936) 34.

22. Gaudentius of Brescia, *Tractatus VI in Exodum* 50.

Chapter Six
The Easter Night

The Jewish Background

"WHY IS THIS NIGHT DIFFERENT FROM ALL OTHER NIGHTS?" THERE IS PROBABLY no question as searching as this ritual question asked by the youngest of the family during the paschal meal. Why the unleavened bread, why the bitter herbs and the roasted lamb? These are not the habitual type of food one would see daily on the table of any Jewish family. These are part of a solemn ritual and they must symbolize something special. To answer the question, the head of the family is instructed by the *Pesachim* to relate the story of their ancestors, their strenuous toil as slaves in Egypt, and their glorious deliverance from bondage. The head of the family is told to explain the liturgical text of Deuteronomy 6:5-9 which narrates the event of the exodus:

> My father was a wandering Aramean who went down to Egypt with a small household and lived there as an alien. But there he became a nation great, strong, and numerous. When the Egyptians maltreated and oppressed us, imposing hard labor upon us, we cried to the Lord, the God of our forebears, and he heard our cry and saw our affliction, our toil, and our oppression. He brought us out of Egypt with his strong hand and outstretched arm, with terrifying power, with signs and wonders; and bringing us into this country, he gave us this land flowing with milk and honey.

The miraculous event of the Passover night when Yahweh struck down all the firstborn of Egypt but spared his own people became the centerpiece of the paschal meal celebration. This night Yahweh "did all these wonderful things for us and our ancestors, and led us from slavery to freedom, from sorrow to joy, from mourning to rejoicing, from darkness to great light, from slavery to salvation."[1] The night of the Passover is thus the culmination of the entire year, the night which devout Jews long to celebrate and for which they make punctilious preparations. On this night they bless Yahweh "who saved us and our ancestors in Egypt and has allowed us to reach this night."[2]

But the exodus is not the sole event commemorated in the paschal night celebration. The exodus is, of course, the principal theme of the feast and its immediate occasion. But it is best understood in relation to the theme of cosmogony. The God who revealed himself during the exodus as the Savior of Israel is none other than the Creator of the universe himself. In the Old Testament as also in the paschal night liturgy the two themes of creation and exodus are so closely bound together, that Isaiah 51:9-10, Jeremiah 32:17-44, and Nehemiah 9:6-36 present them together as if they were one dramatic act of God. Second Isaiah pleads to Yahweh to "awake as in the days of old, in ages long ago! Was it not you who crushed Rahab, you who pierced the dragon? Was it not you who dried up the sea, the waters of the great deep, who made the depths of the sea into a way for the redeemed to pass over?" Creation and exodus merge to form God's saving act of creation or, one might also say, God's creative act of salvation. Indeed, "just as the creation points forward to the exodus and the making of the covenant, so the covenant faith reaches backward and includes creation.[3]

The blending of these themes in the night of the Passover is skillfully accomplished by the poet who wrote the *Four Nights* which is preserved in the Palestinian Talmud.[4] The poem is a targum on Exodus 12:42 which commemorates the "night of vigil for the Lord, as he led them out of the land of Egypt." Although the poem distinguishes four eminent nights written in the "Book of Memorials," it sums them up in the end as a single night, "the night of the Passover to the name of Yahweh, the night that has been set aside for the salvation of all the generations of Israel." As biblical scholar N. Füglister has significantly pointed out, "Judaism regarded a whole series of other saving events in the Bible as Passover events, so that Passover became increasingly a compendium of salvation history."[5]

tttS-128/8H
foram

The first night was the night of creation, "when Yahweh revealed himself over the world to create it." The second night recalls the fulfillment of Yahweh's promise to Abraham, who was one hundred years old, and to his wife Sarah, who was a woman of ninety years, that they would be the parents of a great nation; Isaac was born and at the age of thirty-seven was led to the mountain to be sacrificed. The third night was the night of the Passover and the exodus, "when Yahweh revealed himself against the Egyptians at midnight: his left hand slew the firstborn of the Egyptians while his right hand protected the firstborn of Israel." The fourth night is the night of messianic salvation "when the world reaches its end to be redeemed." The four nights mark the principal stages of God's plan of salvation, namely the creation of the world, the promise to Abraham and Sarah that they would be the parents of the chosen people, the feast of Passover and the event of the exodus from Egypt, and the advent of the messianic age. It should not cause astonishment that the poem calls the four nights "the night of the Passover," for in the mind of the poet everything that God has done and will still do has something to do with the salvation of his people.

In its historicized form the Jewish paschal meal became the yearly solemn commemoration of the wonders Yahweh did for his people, when he delivered them from Egypt with a mighty hand. The meal perpetuates year after year the memory of the exodus. According to a rabbinic tradition based on Exodus 12:14 and 13:3's concept of *zikkaron*, perpetuating the memory of the exodus is not a mere calling the event to mind. The paschal meal is the ritual actualization of God's work; it transports the event of the exodus to the present, in such a way that every Jew can personally experience it. In the words of the Babylonian *Pesachim*, "in every generation everyone is obliged to consider oneself as one of those who departed from Egypt."[6] Through the ritual meal both event and salvation of the exodus will become an object of experience for the Jew, provided he or she participates in the meal and incites the same dispositions as the ancestors had when they celebrated the feast in Egypt.[7]

Describing four types of children who inquire about the ceremonies of the paschal meal, Rabbi Hiyya says of the nonconformist:

The impious child asks, What ceremonies do you perform, and why do you impose this observance every year? Since he excludes himself from the observance, he should be answered thus: It is because God granted great favors to me. But he has not granted them to this impious child who, if he had been in Egypt under Moses, would not have deserved to be delivered from that land.[8]

Participation in the paschal meal requires personal involvement, and personal involvement requires the conviction of faith that what God has done in the past in favor of his people he continues to do today. Without this type of participation no Jew can consider himself or herself a free person; without it he or she still languishes in Egypt.

The *Pesachim* supports its teaching with the instruction of Exodus 13:8 that the ritual should be explained to the child: "On this day you shall explain to your son, This is because of what the Lord did for me when I came out of Egypt." The post-exilic Deutoronomist is sometimes censured as an haphazard editor of earlier legislative codes. Actually he regards the laws and regulations handed down by Moses as a body not so much of historical as of present-day legislations addressed to his readership, his contemporary fellow Jews. Deuteronomy 16:1-8, which regulates the feast of the Passover, makes it evident that the post-exilic Jews are themselves led out of Egypt when they eat the paschal meal. With profound catechetical insight he takes utmost care to establish some kind of contact between his readers and the event of the exodus. You also, he tells his contemporaries, come out of Egypt every year, when you celebrate the Passover feast. The paschal meal is a reminder, for "as long as you live, of the day of your departure from the land of Egypt."[9]

The Night of Creation and Salvation

The themes of creation and exodus are nowhere so highly exalted in Judaism as during the night of Passover and in Christianity as during the night of Easter. We should note, however, that in Christianity these two themes underwent a process of reinterpretation. Creation and exodus are now viewed in the light of Christ's passover and his followers' participation in it. Although early Christian writers made a remarkable effort to link the Old Testament themes with the Christian mystery through the ingenious use of cosmogonic language, they paid little attention to the original meaning of these themes. And rightly, since Christianity viewed them as mere foreshadowing of the spiritual reality of a new birth and salvation in Christ. Nevertheless, the Jewish tradition of regarding creation and exodus as one divine act found echo in the patristic doctrine that rebirth and salvation are one reality.

Gregory of Nazianzus attaches a decidedly Christian and deeply spiritual meaning to the Old Testament themes of creation and exodus. In an homily he delivered on Easter night he focused on the creation of a spiritual world in Christ and our deliverance from sin and the power of the devil.[10] The language he employs, however, has strong cosmogonic evocation, as the following lines will show.

> The resurrection of Christ brought forth this sacred night, which is the enemy of the night of this world. It is the sacred night that dispels the primordial darkness, restores everything to light, form, and order, and transforms the chaos of sin (akosmía) into the cosmos of divine grace.

In another homily Gregory calls Easter the second creation. Like the first, it commenced on the night between Saturday and Sunday, that is, the moment when God began to create the world and when Christ rose from the tomb.[11]

The practice of baptizing candidates on Easter night provided the link between the themes of baptismal photismós or enlightenment and redemption. Pseudo-Epiphanius ponders over this connection in an homily on the resurrection of Christ.[12] On the night of Christ's resurrection from the tomb and our ascent from the baptismal font the light of a new faith, new law, and new people of God shone on the face of the earth. Israel celebrated the Passover at night and crossed the sea at night. We too celebrate Easter at night and cross the water of baptism at night.[13] "But how great is the difference between their Passover and our Easter, between the figure and the truth!" For now "we celebrate in light and splendor," and the water of baptism shines with the light of the Holy Spirit.

We meet this kind of paschal typology notably in the writings of St. Ambrose of Milan.[14] In an address to neophytes he explained how their baptism on Easter night was foreshadowed by the crossing of the sea at night by the Israelites. He recalled how Moses led them at night by a column of light, and during the day by a column of cloud. "What does the column of light signify," he asked, "but Christ the Lord who dispelled the darkness of unbelief and infused the light of truth and grace in the human spirit? On the other hand, the column of cloud refers to the Holy Spirit."[15]

For Ambrose baptism is not only a paschal sacrament but also a sacrament of the new creation. Baptismal typology reaches farther back to the creation of the world. Thus Ambrose reminded the neophytes that the water in which they were immersed at baptism had been prefigured by the water of creation. The primordial water gave life to living things, "but it was reserved for you, that water should regenerate you to grace."[16] When God created the universe, the Spirit hovered over the water. If he hovered over the water, it was in order that it might bring forth life. We have more reason to believe that when the Holy Spirit is invoked over the baptismal font, he comes on the water so that it might signify the reality of our rebirth.[17] On the basis of this typology Ambrose called baptism *vetus mysterium*, an ancient sacrament whose roots extend to the origin of the world.

St. Augustine of Hippo used extensively the creation pericope to illustrate the concept of baptismal *illuminatio* or spiritual purification and enlightenment. In his Easter homilies he often had recourse to the action of the Spirit on the primordial waters and to the first apparition of light, in order to explain what had happened at the Easter night baptism. "Last night," he recalled, "the Spirit of God hovered over the water. There had been darkness over the abyss, while these infants [or neophytes, mostly adult] bore their sins. But after their sins had been remitted through God's Spirit, God said, Let there be light, and there was light."[18] The second creation, like the first, happened at night. And just as at the beginning of time the power of God produced light, so on Easter night baptism dispelled the darkness of sin that lurked in the hearts of catechumens. Augustine repeats this typology in another homily: "There was darkness over the abyss before the sins of the catechumens were forgiven. When these descended to the water over which the Spirit of God hovered, the night of sin was dispelled."[19]

Full Moon and the Easter Candles

Light is a powerful and fascinating symbol, not only of conscious thought, but also of life and salvation. We have seen early on that the symbol of paschal life and salvation is the full moon that rises on 14 Nisan. After the Council of Nicea fixed the feast of Easter on Sunday after 14 Nisan, the light of the full moon was increasingly substituted by the light of Easter candles and lamps. A waning moon was hardly a symbol of the fullness of redemption. The twenty-four hours of continuous light did not always come from the coalescence of the sun and the full moon but, on several occasions, from the succession of lights coming from the sun and the Easter candles and torches that lighted up at night the cathedrals and town squares. Eusebius of Caesarea tells us that Emperor Constantine, though he was only a catechumen, "converted this Easter vigil into divine splendor by the huge torches which he ordered to be lighted throughout the city."[20]

The shift of focus from moonlight to candlelight heightened the symbolic character of the Easter candles. We note in passing that there were two types of Easter candle used in the liturgy. The first type was used in connection with the baptismal procession. The second was the *cereus paschalis,* which originated in the *lucernarium,* the evening rite of lighting lamps at home and later in basilicas. The more solemn form of the *cereus paschalis* is what is known today as the Easter candle.[21] The importance given by the early church to the lighting of candles and lamps at the Easter Vigil reveals its attachment to the patristic tradition of twenty-four hours of continuous light brought by the resurrection of Christ. It underlined the duty of those who have been enlightened in the water of baptism by the Spirit to live always as sons and daughters of light.[22]

We mentioned the use of candles for baptismal procession. The symbolism of this rite did not escape the attention of St. Gregory of Nazianzus. In one of his Easter Sunday homilies he dwelt at some length on the symbolism of the preceding night's torch procession held by the magistrates and townspeople in honor of the neophytes. That *photagogía,* Gregory recalled, illumined the dark night with generous light. The earth became as radiant as the firmament because of the streets that glittered with countless lights. He saw in the brilliance of that night a reflection of the heavenly light of angels, or perhaps of the Blessed Trinity itself which is the source of every created light. Ultimately, however, the *photagogía* on the occasion of Easter baptism signified the light of the risen Christ and the *photismós* or spiritual enlightenment of the newly baptized.[23]

The substitution of the light of the full moon was a process that did not come about suddenly. For instance, it took St. Gregory of Nyssa some time to awaken to the fact that the patristic tradition of twenty-four hours of light rarely involved the full moon and, as a result, a substitute had to be found. In his fourth Easter homily he remarked that the light "which our eyes behold is provided for us tonight by the density of fire coming from the lamps."[24] The night has been transformed into a bright day, the day which the Lord has made. He admitted that "this bright night has made one continuous day, without the interruption of darkness, thanks to the light of the lamps that mingles with the early rays of the sun." In his first Easter homily Gregory spoke of the twenty-four hours of light in relation to the full moon:

> Before the rays of the sun totally disappear, the moon rises on the other horizon to shed its light on the world. Before the moon completes its night journey, the brightness of the sun already mingles with the moon's remaining light. Darkness is thus completely absent on the night of the full moon because of the uninterrupted succession of the sun and the moon.[25]

Was there really full moon on the Easter night of that year, or was Gregory repeating a traditional theme from memory?

We observe a significant change of perspective in Gregory's fourth homily, although its content and language are evocative of the first. The change must have been caused by an increased awareness that the long-venerated 14 Nisan was no longer observed and that the full moon was rarely, if at all, seen during the Easter night. Nonetheless, Gregory did not altogether abandon the treasured Easter theme of a night made as resplendent as the day. The countless lamps burning in the house of God throughout the night compensated, to a measure, for the absence of the full moon.

In the Latin world the symbolism of Easter candles as subtitutes for the full moon was remarkably developed by St. Augustine in his Easter Vigil homilies. He told his congregation that the burning lamps in church not only served the practical purpose of lighting up the church for the vigil and keeping them awake; they also carried a special message. "This holy solemnity," he said, "removes night from this night and by means of these lighted lamps put the darkness to flight."[26] In the thinking of Augustine night and darkness often signify sin and the power of evil, while day and light mean faith, work of justice, and holiness of life.[27] In this sense the lamps symbolized the scattering away of the dark forces of sin and the rising of the light of Christ in the hearts of the redeemed.

Augustine dwelt again on this symbolism in another Easter homily addressed to the people of Carthage:

May God who ordered light to shine in the darkness, shine in our hearts, so that we may do within ourselves what we similarly have done in this house of prayer lighted up with lamps. Let us therefore adorn our consciences, as the true house of God, with the light of justice.[28]

On another Easter night he exhorted his congregation:

As we, enraptured, behold with the eyes of our body the splendor of these burning lamps, let us consider with the eyes of faith the true reason for this glorious night.[29]

On yet another occasion Augustine encouraged the congregation "to solemnly keep vigil against the sleepiness of the body, through these lamps burning in the night. But against the torpor of the heart in the night of this world, let us become lamps ourselves."[30]

Augustine, however, did not neglect the symbolism of the full moon. When the occasion presented itself, and the moon was bright, he acknowledged it in his homiliy by directing the people's attention to the succession of the heavenly lights:

To the vast concourse of people everywhere who are assembled in Christ's name for this sublime feast, the rays of the sun have been lost to view, but the day has not vanished, because a radiant world is now bathed in the light of the heavenly bodies.[31]

The Easter Vigil

In the tradition of the early church the feast of Easter revolves around the Easter Vigil. Until the sixth century this took the form of a nocturnal celebration that began on the evening of Saturday and ended on Sunday at daybreak. A. Nocent has identified the basic liturgical elements of the Easter Vigil in the early centuries. These are the readings from the Old and New Testaments, celebration of baptism and confirmation, and the Eucharist. To these were added in the course of time two other elements that tended to monopolize the attention and imagination of the people, namely the blessing of the new fire and the procession with the Easter candle and the singing of the *laus cerei* or *Exsultet*.[32]

The Easter Vigil had a basic structure which was shared by the great majority of the churches in early centuries. It comprised a prolonged liturgy of the word in the course of which the catechumens received their final instructions prior to baptism, the rite of baptism itself, and the celebration of the eucharist, which concluded the vigil. In Africa in the time of St. Augustine, the first cockcrow, the *gallicinium*, announced the end of the long and tedious hours of psalmody, readings from Scripture, and catechesis. It was dawn: the solemn moment had come for catechumens to be baptized and to participate in the eucharist.[33]

We see in some of Augustine's Easter Vigil homilies the special effort he makes to connect the long night hours of psalmody and readings with the hours when Christ's body lay in the tomb, as well as the celebration of initiation at the early hours of dawn with the resurrection. This probably explains why in the early church the fast was not broken and the sacraments were not celebrated until after the *gallicinium*.[34] For the early cockcrow announced the hour of the resurrection. The joy of this hour, which the Easter season prolonged for fifty days, was expressed through the celebration of the sacraments of initiation.

For his theological depth and his vivid experience of the paschal mystery Augustine holds a place of eminence among early Christians who wrote on the Easter Vigil. For him the "mother of all holy vigils" not only recalls the burial of Christ, it also renders this aspect of the mystery present to the faithful who participate in the vigil. Because the object of the Easter Vigil is the paschal mystery itself, "no other vigil may be compared in excellence to this. The vigil we keep tonight is so special that, even though others bear the name, it alone rightly claims this title."[35] If the vigil is prolonged to several hours of the night, it is to give to the faithful the rare opportunity to keep watch devoutly by the tomb of Christ and thus witness the singular moment when Christ rose from the dead.[36]

A. An Image of the Eternal Vigil

"Why is it that at the yearly recurrence of this feast Christians hold a night vigil? And why do we keep this sublime nightwatch only tonight and not on the night of other feasts as well?"[37] With this question in mind, which is incidentally reminiscent of the ritual question asked by the child during the paschal meal, Augustine sets out to explain the meaning of the Easter Vigil:

> This is the day the Lord consecrated to his glorious resurrection, and tonight, the eve of Easter Sunday, we celebrate the memory

of this event. We pass this night, on which our Lord rose from the dead, in watching and prayer, for it is the night that brought to us a life in which there is neither death nor sleep.

Augustine is careful not to isolate the passion and death from the resurrection:

Having made this day a day of mourning because of his death, our Lord Jesus Christ transformed it into a day of rejoicing because of his resurrection. Now that we solemnly commemorate both events, let us keep watch in memory of his death, and joyfully welcome his approaching resurrection.

In his other Easter homilies Augustine mentions time and again the two aspects of the paschal mystery as the occasion for the vigil.[38] However, he shifts his emphasis from one to the other. Sometimes he focuses attention on the resurrection; at other times on the death and burial.[39] But the impression we get from these homilies is that he generally regards the part of the vigil preceding baptism as the time when the church lives out the hours that Christ spent in the tomb. Those long hours of prayers and hymns, silent reflection, and instructions are timed with the hours when the body of Christ lay in the tomb awaiting the resurrection. With theological depth and insight Augustine declares:

As we keep watch tonight recalling the burial of our Lord, we want our vigil to coincide with the time when he slept for us. Thus on the night when he slept we keep watch, so that by the death he suffered we may have life. We observe a solemn vigil on the night he slept, so that when finally we ourselves shall have arisen for the eternal vigils, we may continue steadfast and unwearied, while he keeps vigil on our behalf. On this same night he arose whose resurrection we now await with longing.[40]

One aspect of the Easter Vigil that Augustine studiously elaborated is its eschatological dimension. In one of his homilies he said: "We assist at the vigil in the very night in which he slept, looking forward to the time, when secure in his watchful care, we shall have no further need of sleep."[41] As we devoutly participate in the vigil, we await the hour of the resurrection and hope that we also shall attain the future resurrection, when "we shall be gathered into his fellowship where we shall no longer sleep nor fall asleep." For Augustine death is symbolized by sleep, and the resurrection by the state of being awake. "For what is death," he asks, "but a long, profound sleep from which God rouses the dead? Where there is no death, there is neither sleep, which is an image of death."[42] Christ whom God roused from the sleep of death dies no more; he is eternally awake, watching over his people. It is this state of eternal wakefulness in the presence of God which we hope to attain.

The thought of a glorified Lord who is always awake and attentive led Augustine to fresher insights on the nature of the Easter vigil. In a manner that is reminiscent of Yahweh's vigil over his people on the night of the Passover, Augustine exhorted his congregation to keep the nightwatch in honor of Christ who now watches over us: *vigilemus ergo vigilanti Christo.*[43] Thus the Easter Vigil evokes or perhaps recreates the night of the Passover in Egypt: "This was a night of vigil for the Lord, as he led them out of the land of Egypt, so on this same night all the Israelites must keep a vigil for the Lord throughout their generations." This passage from Exodus 12:42, according to N. Füglister, shows the mutual character of the Easter watch: "Yahweh watches over Israel during the night, while Israel for its part keeps watch for Yahweh as it waits for him."[44] This is surely what Augustine meant with these words of exhortation: *vigilemus ergo vigilanti Christo.*

In some of his Easter homilies Augustine mentions also the second coming of the Messiah as an occasion for holding the vigil, though he does not affirm that the Parousia will occur on the night of Easter. The imminence of the second coming is an ancient belief, and a number of early Christian writers expected this coming to occur on Easter night.[45] We meet this in a work of Lactantius (d. 330):

> This is the night which we celebrate with a vigil because of the coming of our King and God. There are two reasons for the choice of this night: first, after his suffering he rose from the dead on this night; and second, he shall receive the kingdom of the world also on this night."[46]

St. Jerome saw and lamented the abuses generated by this belief.[47] Some people left the church before the vigil was over and began feasting, because if the Parousia did not take place that night, it would not during the rest of the coming year. Jerome blamed the Quartodecimans for propagating this dangerous belief. For according to them, "Christ will come at midnight, just as God came at midnight in Egypt." Such belief is, of course, consonant with their Easter theology. But in the fourth century it caused great anxiety among the faithful as the Easter night approached, and a reckless sense of relief when the Parousia did not happen. With the passing of centuries the imminence of the Parousia gradually faded into the far-distant future, though the liturgy has never totally lost sight of it. Augustine was surely aware of this belief, but he ignored it in his homilies. Instead, he explained that the church always keeps watch, with the eyes of faith intent on holy Scriptures, while the world, like a night, runs its course until the Lord comes.[48]

B. Easter Vigil: Presence in Mystery

St. Augustine devoted a great deal of his time explaining to the congregation the intricate concept of Easter Vigil anamnesis. When we read the homilies of Augustine, we need to bear in mind that they were not addressed to a group of scholars but to an assembly of townspeople struggling to keep awake through the long nightwatch. We should not thus expect the use of precise technical vocabulary. Indeed, to do so would be to accuse the great preacher of lack of pastoral consideration.

In his homilies Augustine did not, of course, use the word anamnesis. It would have been as strange then as it is today outside the circle of theologians and liturgists. He used instead the word *memoria* (commemoration) or the double negatives *non oblivisci* (not to forget) and *non praeterire memoriam* (not to let the memory pass by).[49] Used in the context of the Easter Vigil, *memoria* suggests a particular meaning which is often difficult to determine. That it does not refer here to a simple commemoration of an historical event Augustine briefly explains in a letter to a certain Januarius.[50] The addressee wanted to know why, unlike Christmas, Easter is not celebrated on a fixed date in the calendar. Augustine replied that there is a basic difference between the two feasts. The birthday of Christ, unlike his resurrection, "is not celebrated in mystery (*in sacramento*)." The event is merely remembered, commemorated. To celebrate *in sacramento*, Augustine explains, is to recall a past event in such a way that another reality is signified and witnessed. What that other reality is, he does not elaborate. But he assures Januarius that this is not the way we celebrate Christmas. On the other hand, "we celebrate Easter in this way, so that when we recall that Christ died and rose again we do not, for reason of signifying the mystery, omit those elements that relate to the event."

Easter is celebrated in mystery, while Christmas is not. Easter, unlike Christmas, has elements that relate to the mystery which is celebrated. These we should not discard from the celebration of the feast. Augustine does not tell us what they consist of, but considering the nature of the inquiry regarding the date of Easter, we can point in all probability to the elements which constitute the date and signify, in their own way, the mystery or event of Christ's death and resurrection. In fact, apart from such elements the feast of Easter loses its character as a yearly celebration, as an anniversary. But since they depend on the movable cycle of the moon, the feast of Easter cannot be fixed on a definite calendar date. The bottom line is that Easter is an anniversary, while Christmas is not.

Hence, the Easter Vigil as *memoria* connotes more than a simple commemoration of Christ's death and resurrection. It is a symbol or sacrament indicating the presence of the paschal mystery to the participating assembly of the faithful. This is what the great Easter theologian Odo Casel termed *mysteriengegenwart*, the presence of the saving events in mystery or in the church's liturgical action through ritual memorial or anamnesis.[51] Just as the Jewish Passover celebrated the actuality of the exodus whereby Yahweh saved his people, so now the feast of Easter celebrates the actuality of Christ's saving mystery. Augustine was keenly attentive to the implications of this doctrine, which already in his time began to give in to a more historical orientation of feasts in view of the introduction of the other phases of Christ's life. As his letter to Januarius shows, Augustine insists on the distinction between Easter and Christmas. The distinction is basic, for the former is celebrated in mystery, that is, while it commemorates the event, it signifies the presence of salvation. In short, the Easter Vigil actualizes the paschal mystery, which is properly the transhistorical and saving element of the event. Augustine expresses this thus in one of his Easter homilies: "Let us keep in mind the past events, so that during this vigil we may also experience (*figuremus*) something of what we celebrate in faith."[52]

The doctrine of presence in mystery permeates the Easter homilies of St. Augustine. Whenever he speaks of the death and resurrection of Christ, he presents them not as mere events of the past, but as actual sources of salvation for those who take part in the celebration. He is careful, however, not to fall into the pitfall of an eternal return.

Time and again he warns his congregation not to imagine that the Lord is awaited during the vigil, "as if he were still to rise from the dead."[53] In one homily he reiterates the doctrine, inspired by Romans 6:9, with greater emphasis: "Our Lord's passion, as we know, happened but once; Christ died once, the just for the unjust. And we possess it as certain and hold it with unshakable faith, that Christ, rising from the dead, dies no more, and death shall no longer have power over him."[54]

The presence of the paschal mystery in the liturgy is not repetition in the strict sense of the word. According to Augustine, it is renewal. To clarify this intricate subject he carefully distinguishes between *veritas* or the event and *sollemnitas* or the ritual memorial which renews the event. In one Easter homily he brilliantly expounds:

> The celebration (*sollemnitas*), which we often repeat, presents in the course of time the event (*veritas*) proclaimed by Scripture with so many proofs to have happened once. Event and celebration do not contradict each other, as if the latter lied, while the former spoke the truth. The event indicates what took place once, while the celebration renews it (*renovat*) frequently in devout hearts. The event points to the past as it in fact happened. The celebration, on the other hand, prevents the past from being lost, not by redoing the event, but by celebrating it (*non ea faciendo sed celebrando*).[55]

The foregoing text reveals the belief of Augustine in the presence, through ritual anamnesis, of the paschal mystery during the liturgical celebration. It reveals too a theological mind striving to reconcile the doctrine of presence in mystery with the pauline *ephapax* or the definitive character of Christ's saving work. The skillful balancing of *facere-veritas* with *celebrare-sollemnitas* is clearly the product of profound reflection. Augustine's thinking on this subject may be formulated thus: in terms of event, the passover of Christ is now history, but in terms of celebration, it is renewed yearly.[56]

Presence in mystery relates not only to the past but also to the future. According to Augustine, the days of Easter are days of rejoicing, because "these days signify everlasting happiness."[57] He underlines the fact, however, that they merely signify it: the heavenly reality is as yet wrapped in mystery (*in mysterio*); it is not yet revealed in actuality (*in effectu*). But the point he wishes to stress is that the celebration of the Easter Vigil embraces the past and the future, so that both become present or actual *in mysterio*. He writes: "The Lord is not crucified when Easter is celebrated. But in the same manner as we signify the past events in the yearly celebration, we also signify the future which is not yet here." Both the past, which is no longer here, and the future, which is not yet here, are signified in the Easter Vigil, that is, they are recalled or anticipated through rites and symbols, and made present in mystery through anamnesis.

Another aspect of Augustine's reflection on presence in mystery is the time element of the celebration. The Easter Vigil coincides with the night hours when Christ's body lay in the tomb awaiting the resurrection. This explains why it is held on this particular night, for it alone of all the nights of the year was able to witness Christ's burial and resurrection. This night, which occurs between the Saturday of his burial and the Sunday of his resurrection, embraces both these mysteries. "Christ's burial," Augustine explains to his assembly, "was prolonged even to this night, so that on this very night should take place the resurrection of that body which was once derided on the cross, but is now adored in heaven and on earth."[58] By noting the flow of the themes of the Easter Vigil from burial to resurrection, Augustine affirmed the unity of the mysteries of Christ.

The manner in which St. Augustine regards the time element of the Easter Vigil is so vivid and realistic, that at times he leaves the impression of entertaining scruples: was Christ still in the tomb at this hour of the vigil, or was he already risen? We meet the same sense of realism, no doubt influenced by his doctrine of presence in mystery, in an homily on Psalm 21: "The yearly remembrance [of the passion] brings before our eyes, in a way, what happened once long ago, and stirs in us the same emotions, as if we beheld our Lord hanging on the cross."[59] One Easter night, after wishing his congregation the joy of the risen Lord, Augustine was seized by a scruple: perhaps at this point in the celebration Christ was not yet risen, perhaps he still lay in the tomb. He solved the problem with the assurance that, "if possibly his body was still in the tomb and had not risen at this hour of our vigil, there is nothing inconsistent in what we do, because he, who died that we might live, slept that we might keep vigil."[60]

A Night Different from Other Nights

The Easter night is different from all the other nights of the year. It was as different for our forebears as it is for us today. It is different, even if the full moon that once symbolized fullness of life has been replaced in the course of time by candles and electric lamps. We normally do not discover a great deal of symbolism in electric lamps, and there is probably no need to. Furthermore, this night is not just different; it is truly unique. And the reason is because on this night the church watches by the tomb of the Savior as it awaits his glorious resurrection. This is the belief that has sustained the tradition of the Easter night. Centuries of Easter controversy did not weaken this belief; rather, the controversy sharpened it as it put the accent on the principle of time concurrence. It means that certain events in life are linked with a particular year, month, day, and hour of day and night. This seems to be the basic principle that governed the celebration of the Easter Vigil during the early church, and we are heirs to it. If we can accept it, we can also understand why the Easter night, why the Easter Vigil.

We stressed the doctrine of anamnesis and presence in mystery in connection with the Easter Vigil. This should not lead us into disregarding the presence of Christ's mystery at other times of the liturgical year. In the theology of several early Christian writers everyday is a feastday, because we are enlightened daily by the word of God and fed daily by the body and blood of the risen Christ. St. Augustine himself admonished his faithful not to hold the Easter days so principally as to neglect the daily feast of the holy eucharist.

Yet throughout the history of Christianity, excluding the Roman West for a period of time, the Easter night was considered the most appropriate time for solemnly commemorating the paschal mystery. Every Sunday, every day, and every hour are surely occasions to experience the presence of Christ's mystery in our lives, but there is only one night in the entire year when the church's solemn memorial of the paschal mystery takes the form of an anniversary celebration. St. Augustine often reminded his congregation to be assiduous in taking part in the "daily Easter celebrations." Nevertheless, he exalted highly the dignity and value of the yearly feast, which "recalls more splendidly, excites more fervently, renews more faithfully" the saving works of the Lord, "as if we beheld them with our eyes."[61]

NOTES

1. *Pesachim, Die Mischna. 3. Traktat,* ed. G. Beer (Giessen 1912) 193-195.
2. *Pesachim* X, 5, *Der Babylonische Talmud* I-III, ed. L. Goldschmidt (Berlin 1930) 665.

3. "Creation," *Interpreter's Dictionary of the Bible*, vol. A-D, p. 727.

4. The text is in R. Le Déaut, *La nuit pascale* (Rome 1963) 64-65.

5. N. Füglister, "The Biblical Roots of the Easter Celebration," in *Celebrating the Easter Vigil* (New York 1983) 9-11.

6. *Pesachim* X, 5, p. 665.

7. J. Schildenberger, "Der Gedächtnischaracter des alt-und neutest. Pascha," *Opfer Christi und Opfer der Kirche* (Düsseldorf 1960) 86-87; see also O. Casel, "Das Mysteriengedächtnis der Messliturgie im Lichte der Tradition," *Jarhbuch für Liturgiewissenschaft* 6 (1926) 140; S. Marsili, "Pasqua ebraica," in *Anamnesis*, vol. 3/2 (Casale Monferrato 1989) 128-135.

8. *Pesachim* X, 4, *Le Talmud de Jérusalem*, ed. M. Schab (Paris 1932) 151.

9. See T. Maertens, *A Feast in Honour of Yahweh* (London 1966) 106-112.

10. Gregory of Nazianzus, *On Holy Easter* II (PG 36:644).

11. Gregory of Nazianzus, *On the New Sunday* (PG 36:612).

12. Pseudo-Epiphanius, *On the Resurrection of Christ* (PG 43:469).

13. Pseudo-Epiphanius also speaks of the water of creation over which the Spirit hovered as a figure of Christian baptism. He identifies this water of the Red Sea and the Jordan where the head of the dragon was crushed; see ibid. Cf. Cyril of Jerusalem, *Catechesis III* (PG 33:441).

14. Ambrose of Milan: *De Sacramentis, De Mysteriis*, ed. O. Faller: *Sancti Ambrosii Opera*, Pars VII, Corpus Scriptorum Ecclesiasticorum Latinorum, vol. 73 (1955).

15. Ambrose, *De Sacramentis* I, 4, p. 20; I, 6, p. 24.

16. Ibid. III, 3, p. 38.

17. Ambrose, *De Mysteriis* 3, p. 92.

18. Augustine of Hippo, *Sermo CCXXVI* (PL 38:1099).

19. Augustine, *Sermo CCLVIII* (PL 38:1195); cf. *Sermo CCXXX* (PL 38:1103). See C. Lambot, "Une série pascale des sermons de Saint Augustin sur les jours de la création," in *Mélanges offerts à Mlle. Chr. Mohrmann* (Utrecht 1963) 213-221.

20. Eusebius of Caesarea, *De Vita Constantini* IV, 22 (PG 20: 1169).

21. G. Benoit-Castelli, "Le Praeconium Paschale," *Ephemerides Liturgicae* 67 (1953) 309-334; J. Pinell, "Vestigis del lucernari a Occident," *Liturgica Montserrat* I (1956) 91-149; Pinell, "La benedicció del ciri pasqual i els seus textos," *Liturgica Montserrat II* (1958) 1-119; P. Jounel, "The Easter Cycle," in *The Church at Prayer*, vol. 4 (Collegeville 1986) 37-38; A. Nocent, "Il triduum sacrum," in *Anamnesis*, vol. 6 (Genoa 1988) 97-103.

22. For patristic association of light with the resurrection of Christ, see Melito of Sardis, *On Easter* 76 and 122; Gregory of Nazianzus, *On Holy Easter* II (PG 36:625); Pseudo-Epiphanius, *On the Resurrection of Christ* (PG 43:465).

23. Gregory of Nazianzus, *On Holy Easter* II (PG 36:644). Etheria describes a baptismal procession in Jerusalem on the eve of Easter; see *Itinerarium Egeriae* XV, 5, Corpus Christianorum Latinorum, vol. 175 (1965) 56.

24. Gregory of Nyssa, *On Holy Easter* IV (PG 46:681). See J. Daniélou, "Mystique de la ténèbre chez Grégoire de Nysse," *Dictionaire de Spiritualité*, vol. 2 (1953) 1972-1985.

25. Gregory of Nyssa, *On Holy Easter* I, (PG 46:621). Gregory returned to the theme of continuous light in a Christmas letter he sent to a certain Eusebius. The day of the full moon, he pointed out, is a day of uninterrupted flow of light from the sun and the moon; see *Letter IV to Eusebius* (PG 46:1027).

26. Augustine of Hippo, *Wilmart VII*, 4 (PL Suppl. II:722). This and other Easter homilies were edited by G. Morin, S. *Augustini Sermones post Maurinos Reperti*, Miscellanea Agostiniana, vol. 1 (1930); see translation of some homilies in P. Weller, *Selected Easter Sermons of St. Augustine* (New York 1959).

27. See, for example, *Guelferbytanus V* (PL Suppl. II:549); *Addit. ad Wilmart* (PL Suppl. II, col. 740); *Sermo CCXXII* (PL 38:1091); *Lambot 6* (PL Suppl. II:779-7)80; *Wilmart V* (PL Suppl. II:720); *Sermo CCXIX* (PL 38:108); and *Sermo CCXXIII* (PL 38:1092).

28. Augustine, *Addit. ad Wilmart 15* (PL Suppl. II:740).

29. *Guelferbytanus V* (PL Suppl. II:549-552).

30. *Addit. ad Wilmart 17* (PL Suppl. II:741-742).

31. *Guelferbytanus V* (PL Suppl. II:549).

32. A. Nocent, "Il triduo pasquale" 98-103. See also A. Adam, *The Liturgical Year* (New York 1981) 75-84; R. Berger, "Content and Form of the Easter Vigil," in *Celebrating the Easter Vigil* (New York 1983) 36-45; T. Talley, *The Origins of the Liturgical Year* (New York 1986) 47-54; P. Jounel, "The Easter Vigil," in *The Church at Prayer*, vol. 4 (Collegeville 1986) 34-46.

33. P. Weller, "The Easter Rite in Africa," *Selected Sermons of St. Augustine* 28-50.

34. The importance of the *galli cantus* or *gallicinium* in the liturgical celebrations during the patristic period is seen by the many references to it. Egeria writes in her *Itinerarium* (p. 69): "Mox autem primus pullus cantaverit, statim descendet epicopus et intrat intro speluncam ad Anastasim . . . et leget resurrectionem Domini episcopus ipse." The reading of the gospel of the resurrection, *ac si per pascha*, is an indication that the hour of cockcrow was regarded by the early Christians as the hour of the resurrection. The *Constitutiones Apostolorum* attaches several meanings to the *gallicinium*: the second coming of Christ (VIII, 31, 5), the "coming of the day for the accomplishment of the works of light" (VIII, 34), the end of the fast (V, 18, 2). Until the fifth century it was the normal practice of the churches not to celebrate baptism on Easter night until after cockcrow; see "Gallicinium," *Dictionnaire d'archéologie chrétienne et de liturgie*, vol. 6 (1924) 593-596.

35. Augustine of Hippo, *Guelferbytanus V* (PL Supp. II:549).

36. See A. Wilmart, "Easter Sermons of St. Augustine," *Journal of Theologi-*

cal Studies 27 (1926) 337-356; S. Poque, *Augustin d'Hippone, Sermons pour la Pâque*, Sources chrétiennes, vol. 116 (1966), introductory notes.

37. Augustine of Hippo, *Guelferbytanus* V (PL Suppl. II: 549-552).

38. Cf. *Guelferbytanus* IV (*PL* Suppl. II:548-549); *Wilmart* IV (PL Suppl. II:717); *Wilmart* IX (*PL* Suppl. II:724).

39. Cf. *Guelferbytanus* IV (*PL* Suppl. II:549); *Guelferferbytanus* V (PL Suppl. II:549); *Guelferbytanus* VI (PL Suppl. II:552); *Wilmart* VI (PL Suppl. II:720); *Sermo CCXX in Vigiliis Paschae* II (PL 38:1098).

40. *Guelferbytanus* IV (PL Suppl. II:549).

41. *Wilmart* VII (*PL* Suppl. II:723).

42. *Guelferbytanus* V (PL Suppl. II:549-552); *Guelferbytanus VI* (PL Suppl. II: 552).

43. *Wilmart* VII (PL Suppl. II:722-723).

44. N. Füglister, "The Biblical Roots of the Easter Celebration" 9-10.

45. Ibid. 26-30.

46. Lactantius, *Divinae Institutiones* VII, 19, Corpus Scriptorum Ecclesiasticorum Latinorum, vol. 19, p. 644.

47. Jerome, *Commentarium in Matthaeum* IV, 25 (PL 26:184).

48. Augustine of Hippo, *Wilmart* IV (PL Suppl. II:717).

49. The homilies where Augustine frequently uses these words are: *Guelferbytanus* IV and V, *Wilmart* VI, VII and IX, and *Sermo CCXX*.

50. Augustine, *Epistola ad Ianuarium* I, 2, Corpus Scriptorum Ecclesiasticorum Latinorum, vol. 34 (1898) 170.

51. O. Casel, *Das christliche Kultmysterium* (Regensburg 1960) esp. 173-75; Casel, "Art und Sinn der ältesten christlichen Osterfeier," *Jahrbuch für Liturgiewissenschaft* 14 *(1938)* 46-53; see S. Marsili, "La liturgia presenza di Cristo," *in Anamnesis*, vol. 1 (Casale Monferrato 1979) 92-96.

52. Augustine of Hippo, *Wilmart* IV (PL Suppl. II:717).

53. Ibid.

54. Augustine, *Enarrationes in Ps. XXI, Sermo 2*, Corpus Christianorum Latinorum, vol. 40 (1952); English translation: S. Hebgin-F. Corrigan, *St. Augustine on the Psalms*, Ancient Christian Writers, vol.29, 1, p. 207.

55. *Sermo CCXX* (PL 38:1089); cf. "Quod enim semel factum in rebus veritas indicat, hoc saepius celebrandum in cordibus piis sollemnitas renovat"; cf. also *Wilmart* IV (PL Suppl. II:717): "In ea [vigilia] renovatur anniversaria sollemnitate memoria Salvatoris."

56. *Sermo CCXX* (PL 38:1089). The following text expresses the doctrine succinctly: "Cogitando quae sunt in memoria, notis temporibus non cessant celebrare sollemnia."

57. *Sermo CCLII* (PL 38:1179).

58. *Guelferbytanus V (PL* Suppl. II:549).

59. *Enarrationes in Ps XXI, Sermo 2*, p. 207.

60. *Guelferbytanus V* (PL Suppl. II:549).

61. *Wilmart IX* (PL Suppl. II:724).